# *Strategies*
### *for the*
## *Director of Christian Education*
### *in the*
## *African American Church*

# Strategies
## for the
## Director of Christian Education
## in the
## African American Church

**DR. ONEAL C. SANDIDGE**

**Sunday School Publishing Board**
**Nashville, Tennessee**

ISBN # 0-910683-77-8

Printed in the U.S.A.
Published by Townsend Press
Nashville, Tennessee

# *Dedication*

This book is dedicated to all directors of Christian education and to all pastors and churches who seek to strive for improving their Christian education program. Special recognition goes to my mother, Hattie Dawson Sandidge; my wife, Janice Oliver; our children: Jermaine Oneal, Ieke Monique Sandidge and godson, Rev. Ronnie A. Clark.

It is also dedicated to all friends and family members who support the Lord's work.

# What Educators Are Saying About
## *Strategies for the Director of Christian Education*

*"The field of African American History continues to grow year after year. New studies about the family and communities serve to broaden our picture of what the African American experience has really been about. Now a new study appears about the Sunday school movement, and how this fits into the complex story of blacks in America. Much can be gained from this primary study."*

Lucious Edwards, Jr., University Archivist—Special Collection Division, Virginia State University, Petersburg, VA

*"Much time and effort have gone into the completion of this work, the contents of which should be beneficial to anyone interested in the history of African Americans in general, and the African American church in particular. Much of the history of the black church remains unwritten, and most of the written history is scattered and not documented, present in libraries, or records have been lost to fire or other causes. Frequently no records were kept. Therefore, Dr. Sandidge was required to travel and search for information in any place that it could be found. This book fills a critical need for information on the history of the black church and the black Sunday school in particular. Black churches, you are urged to research your histories and documents for as much information as possible. Much of this information has already been lost; we cannot afford to lose more."*

Clairborne Shelton, Ph.D., Virginia State University, Petersburg, VA

*"Dr. Oneal Sandidge has a great burden to help his people. He is able to put his knowledge and experience in writing in such a way to offer a lot of practical help to African American churches. This book will especially help directors/ministers of education, but also help pastors and Christian Education Board members. The material is very practical and will immediately help those involved in Christian education."*

Dr. Frank Schmitt, Professor of Christian Education, Liberty Baptist Theological Seminary, Lynchburg, VA

# Contents

**Chapters**

**Appendixes**

# Foreword

## By Dr. Maria Harris

There is passion in this book: for education, for excellence, and most of all, for African American church education. The book is not only for readers and educators who are African American, but also for all who would understand the richness of a contribution and a history hidden too long. It is for readers and practitioners who strive for excellence and understanding in their own educational work.

The author leads us into this understanding and excellence in many ways. First, he creates a **Framework**. Second, he uses numerous **angles of vision** to enable us to see what he sees. Finally, throughout the book, he acts as our **teacher**, subtly instructing us by the many ways he goes about presenting the materials. In this introductory foreword, I shall comment on each of these, even as I recognize that I could have chosen many other ways of working that he uses as he—and the Lord—helps us to explore the vocation of director of Christian education in the African American church.

**The Framework**. To paint a picture of the work involved in directing Christian education, Dr. Sandidge opens and closes the book by alluding to two women. He begins the work by reminding us of Margaret Burroughs' wonderful question, "What Shall I Tell My Black Children?" setting the stage for what is to follow. And to finish, he closes with the poetic story of another African American woman who asked the question, a woman named Katie Ferguson who is noted as a pioneer and mother of the African American Sunday school, dating back to 1793. In the book's middle chapters (chapters three, four, five and six), he engages the reader with the wide range of activities that are demanded from the director of Christian education, although first he situates the director's work by a thorough study of the history of Christian education for African Americans in the United States (chapter one) and follows this with an overview of general educational beliefs in Africa, especially in Ancient Egypt (chapter two). In chapter seven, he returns to this story with a further and closing study, this time of the Sunday school as seen through the lenses of English Sunday Schools, American Schools, and most importantly and detailedly

African American Sunday Schools—a study that also celebrates the rich contributions of the different denominations, notably Baptist, Methodist, A. M. E. Zion, Christian Methodist Episcopal and Presbyterian churches. All of this culminates in several suggestions for the twenty-first century (chapter eight) which just may become another book! This strong opening and closing situate the educational work that the author puts before us, never letting us forget the context in which the work of the DCE goes on.

**Angles of Vision.** To the question, "Exactly what is a Director of Christian Education?" Dr. Sandidge responds from many points of view. He speaks as a **herald**, for example, as he singles out those Scripture passages that are foundational in Christian education, those needed to fully understand family life, and still others that draw attention to teachers, to pastors, to priests, to prophets, and to the church as a whole. He speaks as an **administrator**, carefully delineating—in chapter three, for example—everything from how to look at a contract, to how to develop procedures such as ordering supplies, duplicating materials, and printing bulletins. He is both **minister** and **theologian**, attuned to tradition: the tradition of the local church in which the person ministers, and attuned to the churches through the centuries. He is a **creator**, shaping the curriculum from many points of view, even as he is also a researcher, aware that he is not the first to ask curricular questions, but is instead heir to a vast array of suggestions in curriculum, many of which he outlines for the teacher. He is a **sociologist** and at times a **psychologist**, aware of the human society—and societies—that exist in every church, and aware too of the varying personalities that may characterize the membership of every church. And, as I have already noted, he is an **historian**, delineating the story of the African American church throughout the centuries and bringing us up-to-date as we walk across the threshold of the new millennium.

Teaching: finally, Dr. Sandidge is our **teacher**, aptly suited for the tasks of the Christian educator which are so multiple and manifold, and showing us how both to think about tasks and to engage in them. He instructs in curriculum, as I have already noted, but he reflects on it in such a way that it is not only thorough, but also teaches us about community, human encounter, and personal attitudes. He gives us lists, the core of practicality, that include suggestions as prosaic and specific as getting a large desk calendar for a year, organizing files and cabinets, and studying the church's flow chart; and as far-reaching as working with the superintendent for a schedule of all classes and requesting all ministry leaders to provide a calendar for the events and activities of their ministries. He offers us **models** of the ten super Sunday schools in the church and ways in which the Freemen's Bureau took a role in the origins of the African American Sunday school. He also instructs the reader in setting up the Board or Committee of Christian Education, and then working with the Board—invaluable advice for any DCE.

Such a shorthand description of this book is of course incomplete. Still I hope that I have conveyed some of the excitement I feel when contemplating those who are searching for what Dr. Sandidge offers, and finding it in this book. May his work be blessed, and may he see the fruits of his labor confirmed in the publication of this work and in its adoption by many. And may it be republished from edition to edition serving us all in understanding the high calling that it describes.

(Maria Harris is a distinguished professor, national and international lecturer in Christian education. She is author of many articles and books. Her books include: *Fashion Me a People,* and *Religious Education—Conversations on Contemporary Practice.*)

# Acknowledgments

Special thanks to professors, writers, and others who read part or all of this manuscript. Readers and assistants include Mrs. Janice Oliver and Rev. Ronnie A. Clark. Drafts were read and comments were given by Professor Maria Harris; and, Professor Charles Foster at Candler School of Theology, Emory University, both distinguished authors and professors in Christian education. Special thanks to Ernest Haynes and Arlean Hunter for travel assistance; thanks to Gloria, Joseph, Kim, William, Jr., Rodney and William Oliver, Talithia, Azaael, Barbara and David Slaughter; William and Larry Hunter for special prayers; Patty King, Ph.D. English major at Emory University and Dr. James Campbell, Professor of English at Lynchburg College, for reading manuscript drafts and making editorial suggestions.

## Special Thanks for Assistance in My Research and Writing of Chapter Seven

The Presbyterian Historical Society, Philadelphia Free Library, Pennsylvania, and the American Missionary Fellowship, formerly the American Sunday School Union. Special recognition to Dr. Brenda Hollins at the National Baptist Publishing Board for sharing many insights and providing archival information. I also gratefully acknowledge the help of several colleges and seminaries, such as Howard University, Washington, D.C.; Interdenominational Theological Seminary, Atlanta, Georgia, Virginia Union School of Theology in Richmond, Virginia. David C. Cook Publishing Company assisted in field results. I am thankful for many denominational leaders and pastors, such as the Second Presbyterian Church in New York City; the Gillfield Baptist Church in Petersburg, Virginia and its deacons, Mrs. Lula E. Allgood and Mrs. Thomassine M. Burke as well as their pastor Rev. Dr. Grady Powell; the First Baptist Church in Petersburg, Virginia and her pastor Rev. Dr. Harold Carter and the First African Baptist Church Historian of Savannah, Georgia. I made use of many resources in various archives: Howard University and Schomburg Center for Research in black culture, Harlem, New York; Historian Dr. Stanley Lemons and a Professor of History in a college in Rhode Island; Rev.

Dr. Robert Carter at Congdon Street Baptist Church in Providence, Rhode Island; Dr. Gail Lowe, Smithsonian Institution, Washington, D.C.; Dr. Dennis Dickerson, 13th historian of the African Methodist Episcopal Church, Williamstown, Massachusetts; the Cathedral of St. John Episcopal Church, Providence, Rhode Island; the National Conference of Christians and Jews; and Rebecca Tildesley at the Nathan Bourne Crocker Library in Providence, Rhode Island.

# Introduction

How many times have you asked the Lord to help you survive church work? How many times have you asked the Lord to help the ministry or program of which you were in charge to be not simply a program, but a program that would fulfill God's purpose and meet the needs of the parishioners and community? So many church leaders are perplexed because few people seem ready and available to assist in the work of Christian education. Experience has taught me much about the source of this problem. Over the years, I have grown increasingly concerned about the lack of communication among church leaders.

Some African American church leaders often neglect to pool their resources and to communicate with other leaders in the community and church. Still others are so wrapped up in their titles that they neglect to help one another. Many leaders do not respond to written or verbal communications, or follow up with written confirmations of verbal agreements. Some leaders are willing to lead a ministry, but are not prepared or are unwilling to become prepared for the task; others do not care about their ministry assignment.

One problem in the African American church is the lack of sound administration in the field of Christian education. Contributing to this problem is the lack of understanding regarding why Christian education is important and what Christian education can do for the African American church. The administration of Christian education is often neglected because Christian education is merely seen as an extension of the Sunday church school, when in fact the Sunday church school is an extension of Christian education. Ministries under the Board of Christian Education, including the Sunday church school, need structure, guidance, and direction before leaders and attendees can effectively do their job. This includes understanding the purpose and the objectives of Christian education.

The African American church is progressing, but it still lacks administration in many congregations. This is because leaders often place Christian education in the valley of dry bones, forgetting that help in developing a program is at hand, usually within congregations or sister churches. The African American church must begin to seek training from other Christians, without feeling constrained by denominational ties (e.g., Baptists, Methodists and others). A leader may instruct and offer much assistance without teaching denominational views. For too long the African American church has limited her resources to only those of a certain denomination, a certain church, or a certain community. By taking a more ecumenical approach, and still maintaining denominational views, the African American church can learn to strengthen the administration of its Christian programs.

Christian education is so important to the African American church because it reminds us of our rich teaching heritage. The African American church has always been a teaching church. Some leaders have not viewed it as "Christian" education because emphasis has traditionally been only on the sermon, the Sunday church school, and Bible study. These three are part of Christian education, but so too are all ministries that involve educating. Today, more and more churches are acknowledging the need to have daily and weekly Christian educational ministries.

Christian education helps the African American church to realize why many parishioners seek sources other than the church when struggles appear. Some leaders of Christian education are not prepared because of their limited knowledge about Christian education. A church may have a Christian education program, but if leaders do not know how to develop and implement the program, the program becomes null. Christian education does have an important place in society. Many times, non-Christian educational sources do not provide knowledge for us about spiritual growth, do not help us to understand our desires, and do not help us to cope with our problems.

This book will suggest ideas that will help prepare directors of Christian education for guiding and leading a Christian education program in the African American church. Many suggestions are also helpful to directors serving non-African American churches. This book will also help seminary and college professors, denominational leaders, and directors of Christian education. In addition, this book will provide insights for parishioners in understanding Christian education in the African American church. This book will also help leaders in non-African American churches to learn effective ways to prepare Christian education for African Americans. Christian education is the foundation needed to prepare persons for living. Christian education reminds blacks why education is important. Christian educational programs encourage one to seek further education in public schools, colleges, and theological seminaries. They also increase Sunday church school attendance.

This book consists of eight chapters. Chapter 1 comments on Christian Education for African Americans in the United States; Chapter 2 provides General Educational Beliefs in Africa and Historical Highlights of Education in Ancient Egypt; Chapter 3 refers to the Director of Christian Education; Chapter 4 provides Lists for the Director of Christian Education; Chapter 5 discusses How to Develop a Curriculum in the African American Church; Chapter 6 discusses Organizing a Board of Christian Education and Training Ministry Leaders in Christian Education; Chapter 7 provides Discussions on the English, American and African American Sunday Church Schools; and Chapter 8 offers suggestions for African American Christian Education Programs for the Twenty-first Century. In this book, the term *Director of Christian Education* refers to "Minister of Christian Education." Christian education does much for the African American church. It provides a window for holistic growth from the beginning of one's spiritual growth. It teaches learners that unity among African Americans is important for survival in the African American community.

# What Shall I Tell My Black Children

What shall I tell my children who are black
Of what it means to be a captive in this dark skin?
What shall I tell my dear ones, fruit of my womb,
Of how beautiful they are when everywhere they turn
They are faced with abhorrence of everything that is black?
Villains are black with black hearts.
A black cow gives no milk. A black hen lays no eggs.
Bad news comes bordered in black, black is evil
And evil is black and devil's food is black...

What shall I tell my dear ones raised in a white world
A place where white has been made to represent
All that is good and pure and fine and decent?
Where clouds are white, and dolls, and heaven
Surely is a white, white place with angels
Robed in white, and cotton candy and ice cream
and milk and ruffled Sunday dresses
And dream houses and long sleek Cadillacs
And angel's food is white...all, all...white.

What can I say therefore, when my child
Comes home in tears because a playmate
Has called him black, big lipped, flatnosed
and nappy headed? What will he think
When I dry his tears and whisper, "Yes, that's true.
But no less beautiful and dear?"
How shall I lift up his head, get him to square
His shoulders, look his adversaries in the eye,
Confident of the knowledge of his worth,
Serene under his sable skin and proud of his own beauty?

What can I do to give him strength
That he may come through life's adversities
As a whole human being unwrapped and human in a world
Of biased laws and inhuman practices, that he might
Survive? And survive he must! For who knows?
Perhaps the black child here bears the genius

To discover the cure for...Cancer
Or to chart the course for exploration of the universe.
So, he must survive for the good of all humanity.
He must and will survive.
I have drunk deeply of late from the fountain
Of my black culture, sat at the knee and learned
From Mother Africa, discovered the truth of my heritage,
The truth, so often obscured and omitted.
And I find I have much to say to my black children.

Author—Margaret G. T. Burroughs
(*Used by permission*)

# CHAPTER 1

# Christian Education for African Americans in the United States

T his chapter focuses on Christian education in the African American church. Emphasis is placed on a demo-graphic and historical overview of general education and Christian educa-tion of African Americans in the United States. In order to focus on Christian education in the African American church, it is important to glance at the history of the church, including all of its educational programs. To establish the basis for such a study, let us discuss the African American religious experience based on African life and the subsequent experience of the African American in the United States of America. Within this framework, we can then examine education in the African American church. This chapter offers a brief survey of the African American church from the seventeenth to the nineteenth centuries. In addition to glancing at the Christian education of Afri-can Americans, twelve suggested steps are offered to help the director of Christian education understand the purpose of Christian education in the African American church.

This chapter will allow directors to review facts about education and Christian education of blacks; thus, allowing the director to consider not only the present but also the past when suggesting a curriculum. It will also help directors to think about the future when planning by looking at what the end results of what the curriculum in the African American church should do.

The terms *African American* and *African American church* will be used throughout this book to refer to all people traditionally classi-fied as blacks or Negroes in America, regardless of the shades of their skin color. Similarly, the term *African American church* will refer to that institution or group of Christian denominations owned and oper-ated by people of African descent.

In *Black Theology—A Documentary History*, Dr. Gayraud Wilmore refers to the distinction:

> As applied to religious institutions, Blackness meant the renewal and enhancement of the most esteemed values of Afro-American spirituality, the search for the distinctive norms and characteristics of African and Afro-American religion, the refusal to accept Euro-American theology and church structures as normative. (241)

The African American church, including all African American denominations and African American congregations in predominantly white denominations, is the oldest, largest, and single most influential social institution for African Americans in America (with the possible exception of the African American family, with which the church has an integral relation). A basic profile of African American church strength is necessary to identify the distinctiveness of its focus on education and worship.

The 1999 *African American Desk Reference* reports the following about African American churches. The African Methodist Episcopal Church has 8,000 churches with a membership of 3,500,000; the African Methodist Episcopal Zion Church has 6,000 churches with a membership of 3,000,000; the Church of God in Christ, Inc. has 15,300 churches with a membership of 6,000,000. The National Baptist Convention of America, Inc. has 7,000 churches with a membership of 3,500,000. The National Baptist Convention, U.S.A., Inc. has 30,000 churches with a membership of 7,500,000. The Pentecostal Assemblies of the World has 1,000 churches with a membership of 450,000. The Progressive National Baptist Convention Inc. has 1,800 churches with a membership of 1,800,000.

In a publication for youth curriculum resources entitled "Choosing and Using Resources in the Black Church," Anthony J. Shipley comments about the importance of the learning environment. Christian education in the African American church seeks to create learning environments that include the traditions and life-style of African Americans in order to communicate the message of Jesus Christ (pamphlet). When one looks at Christian education, one is looking at a major element, the Sunday school. These are but a sample of denominational preferences that depict the church-oriented attitudes of African Americans.

The Sunday school is the primary place where people meet to learn about the Word of God. The Sunday school is a major base for providing Christian growth. In *Building a Strong Sunday Church School,* Marcel Kellar states:

> The modern term Sunday school brings together two words: 1. Sunday, the Christian day of worship and reverence in memory of the resurrection of Christ Jesus; and 2. School, which conveys the idea of a modern institution of learning. The total idea and purpose is that a day is set aside when the local congregation comes together to study the Word of God. (4)

Some Christians define the Sunday school as "the Bible teaching arm of the church." In *Reaching the Black Community Through the Sunday School,* Sid Smith states that according to the growth (oriented) approach, the Sunday school is defined as the church organized for outreach, Bible study and ministry. The expectation is to reach people, study God's Word and minister to people (21). This approach, as Smith comments, is the most effective because it seeks to show concern for the whole person.

Christian education provides one with a unique form in the church classroom. Christian education is provided when the Word of God is the chief focus. In *Urban Church Education*, Donald B. Rogers states:

> In the most common forms, that which seems to us to be classic even though its history is relatively short, religious education takes place in a traditional classroom and most often has the intent of handing on the faith. I would say that this is the central form of religious education in our century. It is found in the Sunday school, the parochial school, the CCD Program (Confraternity of Christian Doctrine—a Roman Catholic parish religious educational program) and the Christian day school. In this pattern, students are most often grouped by age or "public school" grade level. The subject matter is Bible, tradition, the elements of worship, cognitive doctrine, the principles of behavior in Christian life, and so forth. (7)

Some white teachers sought to Christianize African Americans who appeared in their presence during slavery. In *Renewing the Sunday School and the CCD*, Mary A. Love speaks, in a chapter entitled "Musings on the Sunday School in the Black Community," about Sunday school growth in the South. African Americans began to reinterpret the Gospel and the task of the Sunday school, causing the development of many local congregations (155).

3

Love demonstrates how the Bible served as a major textbook. The Bible served: to help people to read and write, and to give meaning to and interpretation of the dehumanizing and oppressive situations of slave life. Some African Americans knew how to read the Bible, but others had to listen while others read about the life of the Israelites, the Job story, and the stories about Jesus' ministry and other biblical facts (155). Mary Love also states: " The Sunday school was the place where those first positive concepts of God, Jesus Christ, and nature and mission of the church were experienced and reinforced" (155-56).

## EDUCATION IN THE AFRICAN AMERICAN CHURCH

In examining adult education in the African American church, most records usually refer to both adults and children. It is my task to look at adult education from the 17th to the 19th century.

### CHART ON SOME MAJOR AFRICAN AMERICAN CONVENTIONS AND THEIR ORIGINS

| Name of Body | Date Founded |
|---|---|
| 1. African Methodist Episcopal Church | 1787; 1816 as denomination |
| 2. African Methodist Episcopal Zion Church | 1796 |
| 3. Baptist Foreign Mission Convention | 1880 |
| 4. The American National Baptist Convention | 1886 |
| 5. The National Baptist Educational Convention | 1893 |
| 6. The National Baptist Convention, U.S.A., Inc. | 1895 |
| 7. The Lott Carey Foreign Mission Convention | 1897 |
| 8. The National Baptist Convention of America, Inc. | 1915 |
| 9. The Progressive National Baptist Convention, Inc. | 1961 |

In the journal *Freedom Ways*, Horace Bond discusses in the article "Main Currents in the Educational Crisis Affecting Afro-Americans" that there were many kinds of designations of color for brown or black African Americans, colored people living in America. During the period from 1600 to 1831, African American people were called Africans; from 1831-1880, Colored; 1889-1960, Negro; 1960-1970, Afro-American and black (305). The term "adult education" will designate learning experiences that are inclusive of remedial and advanced education, vocational skills training, personal development programs, and religious instructions. The term "Negro Church" will designate the religious activity of "black" people inclusive of slave meetings, ministries of circuit riders, missionaries, and lay leaders from the 17th to 19th centuries.

The foundation of adult Negro education did not begin in America. In *From Slavery to Freedom*, John Hope Franklin comments that when European traders arrived in Africa, institutions of learning and written languages were already in existence. Youth were taught language through the tribal communities; they learned vocational skills, artisanry, and responsibility from the elders. Tribes specialized in many vocations, such as, agriculture, fishing, basketry, textile weaving, metallurgy, blacksmithing, and woodworking (27).

In *The Education of the Negro Prior to 1861*, Carter G. Woodson writes that on American plantations, owners trained some slaves to be bookkeepers, while Africans developed administrative abilities on a par with their own skills (5-6). Ira Reids writes in the article "Development of the Adult Education for Negroes in the United States" that such training often went beyond bookkeeping and administration. "Their teachers—missionaries of the abolition societies and the socially-minded churches made their errand a religious one—The teaching were based upon the Bible" (300). Forms of vocational training existed on the plantation as slaves learned various skills.

In *Up From Slavery*, Booker T. Washington writes:

> I explained that my theory of education for the Negro would not, for example, confine him for all the time to farm life—to the production of the best and the most sweet potatoes—but that if he succeeded in this line of industry, he could lay the foundation upon which his children and grandchildren could grow to higher and more important things in life. (129)

All of this must be considered in order to understand Negro education as a whole. To better understand Negro education, one can look at African education in the pre-Civil War, in the North and South, and the whole country during Reconstruction.

## Education in the North

Slavery was never as pervasive north of the Mason-Dixon Line as it was in the South, so greater avenues for the education of African Americans were provided in the North. Adults were able to learn in both private and public schools, from their children, and through churches. The free African Americans, who did not want the white way of worship, established independent African American churches.

These independent churches caused African Americans to be alert to an education designed for African Americans, thus evolved a specifically African American process of learning. By taking such a step, they created a process of educating. In *Race, Religion and the Continuing American Dilemma*, C. Eric Lincoln Says:

> The establishment of the black church as an independent institution provided dramatic evidence of black capacity for religious responsibility and the determination to achieve it. . . . For the black believer, the black church was not only a symbol of God's intention that all men should be free, it was also the instrument of God's continuing revelation of that intent. (63)

Africans were involved in educating their people, especially through Sunday school, which provided training in reading, writing, theology, and the liberal arts. According to *The Encyclopedia of World Methodism*, the first independent African denominational church to emerge in America was the African Methodist Episcopal Church (A. M. E.), founded by Richard Allen in Philadelphia in 1787 in response to the racial discrimination Africans experienced in St. George's Methodist Episcopal Church. In 1816, Richard Allen became bishop of branches of this church. Mother Bethel A. M. E. Church, the root of A. M. E. churches, was built in Philadelphia. Part of this facility was a school which provided religious instruction. Not only was faith taught, but reading and writing as well. Then, in 1812, Daniel Coker became a missionary for the A. M. E. Church and established an academy for Africans in Baltimore, Maryland (67).

This view of the A. M. E. Church began to take root throughout America. The A. M. E. Z. Church, founded in New York in the early 1800s, was also active in African adult education and their first church building included a school room (67).

## Education in the South (1620-1831)

In *Religious Instruction of the Negroes in the United States*, Charles Jones reminds us about the South, 1673, in a Christian directory published by Mr. Baxer which included a chapter on "Directions to Those Masters in Foreign Plantations" who had Negroes and other slaves. Mr. Baxer reminds slave owners that God is the absolute owner of slaves and that they should be loved. He also informs the owners to bring slaves to knowledge and the faith of Christ (6-7). Jones states in 1722, in North Carolina, a Mr. Newman baptized 269 children, 1 woman, 3 men and 2 Negroes, who were educated enough to recall the Lord's Prayer, the Ten Commandments, and a creed (12).

The *Encyclopedia of African American Culture and History* informs us that reading and writing was a crime in 1770. Thomas K. Minter and Alfred E. Prettyman remind us: " In 1770, Georgia made it a crime to teach slaves to read and write... " (846). In *A History of Negro Education in the South—From 1619 to the Present*, Henry Allen Bullock discusses a similar crime. He states:

> Despite continued opposition, the practice of training slaves continued to make the plantation what Booker T. Washington called an "industrial school." What was to become one of the most controversial movements in the entire history of Negro education was actually begun within a system officially committed to the policy that Negroes should not be educated at all. (6)

In later years, some states, such as Georgia, had a constitution to protect slave owners. The State of Georgia had a constitution to allow the free exercise of religion with provisions. In *A Documentary History of Education in the South Before 1860*, Edgar Knight informs us that, "All persons whatever shall have the free exercise of their religion; provided it be not repugnant to the peace and safety of the State; and shall not, unless by consent, support any teacher or teachers except those of their own profession" (42). African Americans were restricted in many ways and they had to find other ways to exercise their religious talents, one of which was to provide education in their own families.

In *African Background Outlined*, Carter G. Woodson provides insights about the slaves in the South. Certain owners, however, taught slaves the Bible, especially to the minister and his family, although it was prohibited by law. He states: "Certain masters, too, like Joseph Davis, brother of Jefferson Davis, had slaves trained to be used for special business purposes on the plantation " (339), because African Americans did not know how to read or write. Some African Americans were taught in slave owners' homes. Whites often preached to African Americans using the Bible to justify slavery. The Bible did not uniformly justify slavery; however, many whites have simply selected Scriptures that support their actions. Whites preached from such themes as, "Servants, obey your masters, for it is right in the Lord" (339). They expounded on Scriptures that referred to the curse of Ham. For example, Carter G. Woodson quotes "Cursed be Canaan" or "Japheth shall dwell in the land of Shem and Canaan shall be his servant" (339). Woodson then adds: "The Negroes in these meetings, however, were not permitted to learn to read the Bible" (339).

In considering education in the African American church, one might find that tradition makes it difficult to shift from old ideologies to new awakenings. As Lonzy Edwards suggests, efforts for training pastors with new ideas are usually not accepted overnight.

## 1831 Through Reconstruction

In 1847, the A. M. E. Church published, *The Christian Herald*, later changing its name in 1852 to *The Christian Recorder*, to discuss religious, moral, social, scientific, and literary issues relevant to blacks (102). The publication provides a vehicle for blacks to express themselves and a means to educate other blacks.

In his article, "The A. M.E. Church: A Study of Black Nationalism," Alain Rogers discusses Daniel Payne, one of the black men educated during Reconstruction. He was born to free parents in Charleston, South Carolina in 1811 and received formal schooling for three years until his school was closed because of the uncovering of the Vessey Plot. Payne was inspired by Rev. John Brown of Haddington,

Scotland, and later studied independently. The year of conversion, Payne joined the church and became a member of the A.M.E. Church (28).

After conversion, Payne established a school for black children, having three pupils and three slave students who attended at night to learn reading, writing, arithmetic, and spelling (28).

In spite of such obstacles, some did encourage educational training among blacks who were limited because most slave owners did not want blacks to be educated. One of the most distinguished black advocates of religious education was Bishop Daniel Payne of the African Methodist Episcopal Church. Around 1853, Payne criticized the leadership of some Sunday schools in Philadelphia for leading poor leadership. Then as now, many schools possessed unqualified teachers. Many teachers report to Sunday school when they feel like it, rather than taking the Christian profession as a serious matter. Daniel Payne also informs: "Strive to secure qualified teachers for Sunday schools." Teachers were advised by Daniel Payne to attend a weekly training class and to establish good libraries. He suggested materials such as: a Bible, a Bible dictionary, a history text, biblical geography, a book on self-culture for teachers of psychology, maps and charts. He encouraged Sunday school participants to study. In addition, he advised pastors to preach several times a year on "the duty and necessity of family worship" (28). In the *Religious Education Journal*, Lonzy Edwards states:

> Though the suggestions which Payne made were impressive, it is doubtful, given the controversy over educational requirements in the church, that the clergy was prepared to put them into practice. Nevertheless, by the time the Civil War was over, the African Methodist Episcopal Church, under Payne's leadership, had become involved in the South and probably had trained the personnel required to implement his sophisticated ideas on religious education. (416)

After the Civil War, churches from the North, South, and West cooperated to provide education to African American adults. The African American church has been the unifying force in the lives of African Americans; and since its beginnings, African Americans have been involved in education. The African American church and its religious community must continue to grow and develop (45). In other words, the African American church should continue to educate her people.

In *The Negro Church in America*, Edward Franklin Frazier reminds us of what happened in the New World. He states: "In the New World the process by which the Negro was stripped of his social heritage and thereby, in a sense, dehumanization was completed" (10). African American family values cannot be fully restored because real ancestors are missing from our family trees. The Negro in America lost the traditional African system of kinship which has resulted in broken families. During slavery, there was no legal marriage, and family relationships were temporary and dependent upon the white masters (13).

In order to comprehend the organizational structure and polity within the African American church, this study of the history of African American education as well as the origins of ancient African cultural and religious traditions is important. In *Biblical Faith and the Black American*, Latta Thomas discusses the emerging of the African American church. The author states, "Any word of admonition to the Black church should be prefaced with the reminder that the very existence of a Black church resulted from the fact that American Christianity never fully came to grips with the issues of race in this country" (131).

The author further explains that: "Moreover, the Black church has been the freest institution Blacks have had and perhaps the only one which they could rightly call their own" (134). Still, none of this prevented African Americans from acquiring an education and educating others.

In addition to the African American church, other institutions also educated Negroes in América. Some white churches initiated programs to educate Negroes, and a few slave masters also provided academic training for their slaves, teaching them whatever they wanted slaves to learn.

Christian education does much for the African American church. In *Developing Christian Education in the Local Church*, Nellie B. Moore in her article discusses the needs of Christian education in the black church. She comments: "Christian education is one of the greatest needs of the church and the world" (21). Christian education provides a window for holistic growth. It teaches students that unity is important for survival in the African American community. A Christian educational program helps students to understand that attending church or being a church member is more than listening to preaching; rather, it is being taught what God wants to convey through His preacher. Christians are informed of how the entire Bible is meaningful and should be learned as a part of Christian living. Whenever the man or woman of God stands to preach, they stand to educate as well as to deliver God's divine Word.

Christian education in the African American church is different from Christian education in non-African American churches, because African Americans have experienced oppression in a way no other group has. The problems that beset the African American community are often related to oppression such as low self-esteem, that has been multigenerational for many African Americans, unemployment, and lack of educational opportunities.

The African American church cannot afford to dismiss the fact that she is not doing Christian education. Every African American congregation—whether the bourgesis (those who are middle class, with property-oriented minds), urban and rural congregations (those who have trained and untrained ministers and soul-stirring music), folk congregations (those who are holding on to the old-time or slave religion), and the prophetic congregations (those who are healing in a special way and see the preacher as a prophet)—need to strive toward educating both church and community.

There are many definitions of Christian education, but I would like to share my definition of Christian education. **Christian education may be defined as all education that takes place in the Christian congregation. It is that education supplied by Christians, who in turn are responsible for directing, preparing, cultivating, motivating, illuminating, and convicting students to have a better relationship with God.** This can happen through biblical studies, inspiration from God, a sound curriculum, and faithful leadership.

Christian education equips a Christian to evangelize, and to understand his or her gifts in the church. Christian education teaches students to be Christlike and God-fearing. Christian education prepares the "whole" person for Christian life.

In *Introduction to Biblical Christian Education*, Edward L. Hayes describes the role of the Bible in Christian education in his chapter

"The Biblical Foundations of Christian Education." Christian education "arises from the fertile soil of the Bible" ( 25). The Bible is the foundation for Christian education. In *The Bible in Christian Education*, Iris V. Cully states that: "The Bible is the foundation for Christian education, because through its pages Christians learn who God is and how God acts" (9). The Bible serves as a textbook and a model for living. In the article, "God's Viewpoint of Christian Education," Dr. Benjamin Johnson states: "Christian education is a process of training people to act out what they have been taught from the supreme textbook, the Bible" (5).

In *Building Leaders for Church Education*, Kenneth Gangel provides a list of what a Christian educational program does for the church. Demanding that the church be responsible for the total maturity of its members, he writes:

"The Christian education program of the local church should seek to lead a person to:

1. a biblical understanding of the triune God and a personal relationship with Him through Jesus Christ His Son.
2. a biblical relationship with other Christians in a vital participation with them in the universal church.
3. a biblically constant and thorough program of Christian nurture which has emphasis on doctrine, development of personal Christian convictions, and a scriptural conduct of oneself in family and larger social groups.
4. a biblical recommitment of oneself to Christ in discipleship.
5. a biblical and enthusiastic participation in the witness of the Gospel to the whole world. (44)

The Christian education program should seek to do twelve or more things in the African American church: **Teach the Word of God, teach holistic living, teach rehabilitation from crisis, teach people survival skills, help people understand their identity, teach the purpose for living, teach how to develop true relationships, teach people how to be independent, teach how to pick up the pieces and go on with life, teach African heritage in Scripture, teach African history, and teach Christian education through advanced technologies.** In the following section, I comment on each of these.

The twelve components listed above should be considered when developing education for ministries. A Christian education program must prioritize the Word of God. Every curriculum must include the Word of God. Every ministry meeting should include teaching the Word of God.

## 1. Teach the Word of God

The purpose of ministry meetings is to aid spiritual growth. The Word of God teaches one how to live and how to grow in God's grace. The African American church has always placed emphasis on the Word on the day of worship, during Sunday school, and during Bible study. Equally important is allowing the Word of God to be the foundation for Christian education ministries. Chapter four highlights steps for developing a curriculum.

## 2. Holistic Living

The Christian education program considers the whole person. It considers modern ways for living: reviewing herbal life, massages, physical activities, medical screenings, and recreation, all that help Christians seek alternative healings and be more productive in allowing their dreams to come true. Most of all, when a Christian education program endorses holistic living, one may be physically better able to serve God in body, mind, and spirit.

## 3. Rehabilitation

The Christian education program may discuss rehabilitation, which could provide a wholesome program for rehabilitating people. The first need is to teach sinners how to become Christians. The Christians need to be taught how to remain "saved." This may mean finding ways to give up habits, some of which cause us to sin. They include overcoming drugs, alcohol, sexual behavior, gossip, fear, anger, physical and verbal abuse, backbiting, jealousy, hatred, negative peer pressure, and making our bodies a living sacrifice. The Word of God provides spiritual insights to assist persons in making a commitment to God. The African American church has a concern to help people change. The alcoholic, the drug-user, the mentally disturbed, the possessed, the lonely person, the person recovering from various problems, the persons with unresolved problems that beset the African American community, all need ways to be rehabilitated and return to a spirit-filled life.

## 4. Survival Skills

Part of being independent is seeking survival skills. Survival skills need to be taught in the Christian education department. One needs to understand parenting, including how to be a single parent, how to complete job applications, how to manage personal financial obligations, and how to survive. Many African Americans attend church and yet leave the church with a fuzzy mind because they did not concentrate on the Word of God.

They do not concentrate on the Word of God because they cannot often apply the Word to daily living. When application is reasonable, often one cannot understand the meaning of biblical facts because Scripture often is not exegeted to provide an understanding of the Word. The Christian education program should teach one how to apply the Word as a foundation to seeking survival skills.

## 5. Identity

The African American Christian education program should consider curriculum content that focuses on identity questions such as "Who am I?"

Many African Americans raise questions about the church, her purpose, and the pros and cons of the preacher. They also discuss the lack of church involvement among African Americans which results in some African Americans not being sure who they are.

As a result, some African American church leaders criticize the church for not being able to get its members to participate. When the Christian education program teaches parishioners to focus on self, one can then glance at his or her own deficiencies and then view God as the One who can help achieve all goals.

## 6. Purpose

After helping us understand our identities, "who we are," the Christian education program should provide opportunities for one to look at individual purpose. Why do I exist? How do I know what my purpose might be? How can defining and explaining my purpose become a reality? Some African Americans attend church for years but are unclear about their purpose. The purpose goes beyond spiritual gifts; it is what God has called one to do. Every human exists for a purpose, to serve God and to make disciples. The method or specific calling of an individual is what the Christian education program should address.

## 7. Relationships

Knowing how to survive allows one to have freedom for thinking, enjoying and serving God. Relationships can be better understood when one puts relationships before teaching. The Christian education program should teach one how to focus on self and basic needs. When one is at the moderate level of having his or her basic needs met, one can then focus on relationships. Assuming that one has already created a relationship with God, one can now better interpret the God/I relationship. When the God/I relationship is understood, interpersonal relationships can be taught. The first and most important relationship comes through seeking God and His kingdom.

## 8. Independent

There is much talk about being independent. The African American church can teach one to be independent; that is, how to seek a spiritual life for oneself, how to depend on God for oneself, and how not to blame others for one's actions. The Christian education program can guide one toward developing independence. Self-help skills are very important at this stage. Christian education can offer programs and services to help members of the community to be courageous and independent.

## 9. Picking Up the Pieces

Knowing God and your relationship with God will help you to pick up the loose or lost pieces in life. Picking up the pieces in life is regaining that which you have lost. Some people have lost things such as health, love, finances, morals, and peace within. Picking up the pieces is simply moving on with life. It is taking the good and discarding the bad to have a fruitful life. Part of picking up pieces is considering your entire life.

## 10. African Heritage in Scripture

When one is mentally and physically groomed, one can begin to have deeper insights about Scripture; for example, one begins to see not white people in Scripture, but also people of color: the people who are really represented in most Bible stories. All heritages should be viewed as a whole. African heritage is embedded throughout the Bible. More and more writers are teaching eye-openers about African heritage in Scripture (See Dr. Cain Hope Felder's books for examples). Christian education should re-emphasize these great teachings. The African American church is well on her way to discovering the Gospel truths about biblical events and names. Hopefully, the search of African heritage will cause one to seek more and more truths about African history. For example, one will learn that Moses was "black."

## 11. African History

Many public and private schools do not teach truths about African history, and this is an oversight which we can begin to correct in the church. But others do, such as the African American scholars Dr. James Cone, Dr. Charles Copher, Dr. William Myers, Dr. Thomas Hoyte, Jr., and Dr. Randall Bailey. African history helps one to understand the roots of civilization. When African history is considered, one can begin to review the various ways to share Christian education.

## 12. Christian Education Through Advanced Technologies

Christian education can be accessible through many forms. Advanced technology allows churches to share African history and Christian education facts such as Bible study through web sites on the Internet and provide training and education through the use of computers. The church no longer has an excuse for not providing her best in Christian education. The church should consider the various technologies when revitalizing her program.

# SOME HELPFUL SCRIPTURES FOR
# UNDERSTANDING CHRISTIAN EDUCATION

The Christian educational program has roots in both the Old and New Testaments. Some of these roots are found in the Scriptures listed below. These Scriptures will help you understand why we need to take Christian education seriously. It does not limit one group of people, one race, or one church in its mandate. The African American church must make Christian education relevant to her people.

## Foundational

2 Timothy 2:15

Do your best to win God's approval as a worker who doesn't need to be ashamed and who teaches only the true message.

Acts 13:1

The church at Antioch had several prophets and teachers. They were Barnabas, Simeon, also called Niger, Lucius from Cyrene, Manaen, who was Herod's close friend, and Saul.

Deuteronomy 6:1-9

The LORD told me to give you these laws and teachings, so you can obey them in the land he is giving you. Soon you will cross the Jordan River and take that land. And if you and your descendants want to live a long time, you must always worship the LORD and obey his laws. Pay attention, Israel! Our ancestors worshiped the LORD, and He promised to give us this land that is rich with milk and honey. Be careful to obey Him, and you will become a successful and powerful nation.
Listen, Israel! The LORD our God is the only true God! So love the LORD your God with all your heart, soul, and strength. Memorize His laws and tell them to your children over and over again. Talk about

17

them all the time, whether you're at home or walking along the road or going to bed at night, or getting up in the morning. Write down copies and tie them to your wrists and foreheads to help you obey them. Write these laws on the door frames of your homes and on your town gates.

Matthew 7:28-29

When Jesus finished speaking, the crowds were surprised at His teaching. He taught them like someone with authority, and not like their teachers of the Law of Moses.

Matthew 28:20

And teach them to do everything I have told you. I will be with you always, even until the end of the world.

### Family Education

Family education is a key subject for the African American church. Christian education is not only for individuals, but it teaches the entire family. It helps reunite families, breaks strongholds within families, and suggests ways for bonding families. These Scriptures teach families how to be faithful to the God we serve. They provide a mandate for our Christian obligation to teach the entire family about God.

Deuteronomy 4:9-10

You must be very careful not to forget the things you have seen God do for you. Keep reminding yourselves, and tell your children and grandchildren as well. Do you remember the day you stood in the LORD's presence at Mount Sinai? The LORD said, "Moses, bring the people of Israel here. I want to speak to them so they will obey me as long as they live, and so they will teach their children to obey me too."

Genesis 18:19

I have chosen him to teach his family to obey me forever and to do what is right

| | and fair. Then I will give Abraham many descendants, just as I promised. |
|---|---|
| Exodus 12:26-27 | Your children will ask you, "What are we celebrating?" And you will answer, "The Passover animal is killed to honor the LORD. We do these things because on that night long ago the LORD passed over the homes of our people in Egypt. He killed the first-born sons of theEgyptians, but he saved our children from death." |
| Proverbs 1:8 | My child, obey the teachings of your parents. |
| Proverbs 22:6 | Teach your children right from wrong, and when they are grown they will still do right. |
| Isaiah 38:19 | Only the living can thank you, as I am doing today. Each generation tells the next about your faithfulness. |
| Deuteronomy 11:19 | Teach them to your children. Talk about them all the time—whether you're at home or walking along the road or going to bed at night, or getting up in the morning. |

## Priests

The priests in biblical times had an obligation to teach the Word of God. The following Scriptures remind us about their obligation. Obedience seems to be the key in these texts. Priests or other spiritual leaders provide Christian education in our churches through their obedience to God.

| 2 Chronicles 17:9 | They carried with them a copy of the LORD'S Law wherever they went and taught the people from it. |
|---|---|

| | |
|---|---|
| 2 Chronicles 15:3 | For a long time, the people of Israel did not worship the true God or listen to priests who could teach them about God. |
| Deuteronomy 24:8 | I have told the priests what to do if any of you have leprosy, so do exactly what they say. |
| Deuteronomy 33:10 | You teach God's laws to Israel, and at the place of worship you offer sacrifices and burn incense. |
| Deuteronomy 31:9-13 | Moses wrote down all of these laws and teachings and gave them to the priests and the leaders of Israel. The priests were from the Levi tribe, and they carried the sacred chest that belonged to the LORD. Moses told these priests and leaders: "Each year the Israelites must come together to celebrate the Festival of Shelters at the place where the LORD chooses to be worshiped. You must read these laws and teachings to the people at the festival every seventh year, the year when loans do not need to be repaid. Everyone must come—men, women, children, and even the foreigners who live in your towns. And each new generation will listen and learn to worship the LORD their God with fear and trembling and to do exactly what is said in God's Law." |
| Leviticus 10:11 | You must also teach the people of Israel everything that I commanded Moses to say to them. |

## Teachers in the Church

Teachers in the church are distinguishable from public school teachers, college professors, or any other teacher. These teachers are chosen by Christ. The Holy Spirit helps in selecting teachers. Leaders should pray and be guided when selecting teachers. God knows who should teach. Once selected, the church has a duty to train teachers; the duty has nothing to do with the calling. In other words, because one is called does not mean that one is exempted from training. As a matter of fact, the calling itself should be a primary reason for one to seek training. At the same time, many church members may not be called to teach. Scriptures such as the ones below will enlighten you regarding what the Bible says about teachers. They remind us to exercise the spiritual gift of teaching. More discussion about teachers will take place in chapter seven.

| | |
|---|---|
| Ephesians 4:11 | Christ chose some of us to be apostles, prophets, missionaries, pastors, and teachers. |
| 1 Corinthians 12:28 | First, God chose some people to be apostles and prophets and teachers for the church. But He also chose some to work miracles or heal the sick or help others or be leaders or speak different kinds of languages. |

## New Testament Teachers

Teachers in the New Testament had a serious mandate for teaching. These Scriptures will show and provide you with some classroom observations of New Testament teachers. The church must carefully observe her teachers. The important question is: Does the teacher teach the way of Christ?

| | |
|---|---|
| Acts 2:42 | They spent their time learning from the apostles, and they were like family to each other. They also broke bread and prayed together. |
| Acts 5:25 | Just then someone came in and said, "Right now those men you put in jail are in the temple, teaching the people!" |
| Acts 4:1-2 | The apostles were still talking to the people, when some priests, the captain |

of the temple guard, and some Sadducees arrived. These men were angry because the apostles were teaching the people that the dead would be raised from death, just as Jesus had been raised from death.

Acts 5:18

They arrested the apostles and put them in the city jail.

Acts 11:26;

He found Saul and brought him to Antioch, where they met with the church for a whole year and taught many of its people. There in Antioch the Lord's followers were first called Christians.

Acts 18:25

He also knew much about the Lord's Way, and he spoke about it with great excitement. What he taught about Jesus was right, but all he knew was John's message about baptism.

1 Corinthians 4:17

That's why I sent Timothy to you. I love him like a son, and he is a faithful servant of the Lord. Timothy will tell you what I do to follow Christ and how it agrees with what I always teach about Christ in every church.

1 Timothy 1:3

When I was leaving for Macedonia, I asked you to stay on in Ephesus and warn certain people there to stop spreading their false teachings.

2 Timothy 2:2

You have often heard me teach. Now I want you to tell these same things to followers who can be trusted to tell others.

## Pastors

The role of pastors in Christian education is to teach and see that biblical teaching is the main focus of Christian education. Teaching must include the same subjects that Jesus taught. Pastors must be good teachers and have patience with learners.

1 Timothy 4:11

Teach these things and tell everyone to do what you say.

1 Timothy 3:2

That's why officials must have a good reputation and be faithful in marriage. They must be self-controlled, sensible, well-behaved, friendly to strangers, and able to teach.

2 Timothy 2:2

You have often heard me teach. Now I want you to tell these same things to followers who can be trusted to tell others.

2 Timothy 2:24

And God's servants must not be troublemakers. They must be kind to everyone, and they must be good teachers and very patient.

Ephesians 4:11-12

Christ chose some of us to be apostles, prophets, missionaries, pastors, and teachers, so that his people would learn to serve and his body would grow strong.

## Prophets

Christian education leaders should remember how important it is to hear the prophetic voice. In spite of one's personal agenda, the prophetic voice should dictate our behavior. The prophetic voice is the Spirit of God.

2 Kings 2:3-4

A group of prophets who lived there asked Elisha, "Do you know that today the LORD is going to take away your master?" "Yes, I do," Elisha answered. "But don't remind me of it." Elijah then said, "Elisha, now the LORD wants me to go to Jericho, but you must stay here." Elisha replied, "I swear by the living LORD and by your own life, that I will stay with you no matter what!" And he went with Elijah to Jericho.

| | |
|---|---|
| 2 Kings 4:38 | Later, Elisha went back to Gilgal, where there was almost nothing to eat, because the crops had failed. One day while the prophets who lived there were meeting with Elisha, he said to his servant, "Fix a big pot of stew for these prophets." |
| 2 Kings 6:1 | One day the prophets said to Elisha, "The place where we meet with you is too small." |

## Church

The church of God has always been the mouthpiece for God's Word. The church is more than a place to meet. It also has an agenda to teach. It teaches members how to become disciples. These Scriptures remind us about the church and her assignment.

| | |
|---|---|
| Matthew 28:19-20 | Go to the people of all nations and make them my disciples. Baptize them in the name of the Father, the Son, and the Holy Spirit, and teach them to do everything I have told you. I will be with you always, even until the end of the world. |
| Colossians 3:16 | Let the message about Christ completely fill your lives, while you use all your wisdom to teach and instruct each other. With thankful hearts, sing psalms, hymns, and spiritual songs to God. |
| 2 Timothy 2:2 | You have often heard me teach. Now I want you to tell these same things to followers who can be trusted to tell others. |

| Hebrews 5:12 | By now you should have been teachers, but once again you need to be taught the simplest things about what God has said. You need milk instead of solid food. |

## Holy Spirit

The Holy Spirit is the best teacher in Christian education. The Holy Spirit provides direction for us to plan, teach, and learn about students' past, present, and future needs. There are many instances in the Bible where the term *Holy Spirit* is seen. More than seeing or reading the words, the Christian educator needs to comprehend that the entire Christian education department lies on the foundation guided by the Holy Spirit.

| Isaiah 11:2 | The Spirit of the LORD will be with him to give him understanding, wisdom, and insight. He will be powerful, and he will know and honor the LORD. |

| John 14:16-17 | Then I will ask the Father to send you the Holy Spirit who will help you and always be with you. The Spirit will show you what is true. The people of this world cannot accept the Spirit, because they don't see or know Him. But you know the Spirit, who is with you and will keep on living in you. |

| Ephesians 1:17 | I ask the glorious Father and God of our Lord Jesus Christ to give you his Spirit. The Spirit will make you wise and let you understand what it means to know God. |

| John 14:26 | But the Holy Spirit will come and help you, because the Father will send the Spirit to take my place. The Spirit will teach you everything and will remind you of what I said while I was with you. |

| John 16:12 | I have much more to say to you, but right now it would be more than you could understand. |

## Spiritual Gifts

Christian educators should be familiar with spiritual gifts. Students need to learn how to recognize their spiritual gift(s). The Christian leader knows that others possess spiritual gifts. Once the teacher has recognized spiritual gifts, the next thing to do is to encourage students to exercise those gifts. It is so easy to talk about spiritual gifts, but it is more helpful when one puts the gift(s) into action.

| Romans 12:7 | If we can serve others, we should serve. If we can teach, we should teach. |

| 1 Corinthians 12:28 | First, God chose some people to be apostles and prophets and teachers for the church. But he also chose some to work miracles or heal the sick or help others or be leaders or speak different kinds of languages. |

| Ephesians 4:11-12 | Christ chose some of us to be apostles, prophets, missionaries, pastors, and teachers, so that his people would learn to serve and his body would grow strong. |

| Matthew 28: 19-20 | Go to the people of all nations and make them my disciples. Baptize them in the name of the Father, the Son, and the Holy Spirit, and teach them to do everything I have told you. I will be with you always, even until the end of the world. |

# WORKS CITED

Bond, Horace Mann. "Main Currents in the Educational Crisis Affecting Afro-Americans." *Freedom Ways*. 8:3 (Fall,1968), 305.

Bullock, Henry. *A History of Negro Education in the South—From 1619 to the Present*. Cambridge, Massachusetts: Harvard University Press, 1967.

Cully, Iris V. *The Bible in Christian Education*. Minneapolis: Augsburg Fortress Press, 1995.

Cully, Iris, et al. *Harper's Encyclopedia of Religious Education*. New York: Harper and Row, 1990.

Edwards, Lonzy. "Religion Education by Blacks During Reconstruction," *Religious Education*. 69: (July-August, 1974), 413-416.

Franklin, John Hope. *From Slavery to Freedom: A History of Negro Americans*, Third Edition. New York: Alfred A. Knopf, 1967.

Frazier, E. Franklin. *The Negro Church in America*, New York: Schocken Books, 1974.

Gangel, Kenneth. *Building Leaders for Church Education*. Chicago: Moody Press, 1970.

Harman, Nolan. *Encyclopedia of World Methodism*. Vol. 1. Nashville: United Methodist Publishing House, 1974.

Hayes, Edward L. "The Biblical Foundations of Christian Education" in *Introduction to Biblical Christian Education*. Werner Graendorf, editor. Chicago: Moody Press, 1981.

Johnson, Benjamin. "God's Viewpoint of Christian Education," *The Christian Education Informer*. 50:1. (June—August, 1997), 21.

Jones, Charles. *Religious Instruction of the Negroes in the United States*. New York: Kraus Reprint Company, 1969.

Kellar, Marcel. *Building a Strong Sunday Church School*. Nashville: National Baptist Publishing Board, 1987.

Knight, Edward, editor. *A Documentary History of Education in the South Before 1860*. Chapel Hill: The University of North Carolina Press, 1950.

Lincoln, Eric C. *Race, Religion, and the Continuing American Dilemma*. New York: Hill and Wang, 1984.

Love, Mary A. "Musings on the Sunday School in the Black Community" in *Renewing the Sunday School and the CCD*, edited by D. Campbell Wyckoff. Birmingham: Religious Education Press, 1986.

Minter, Thomas and Alfred Prettyman. *Encyclopedia of African American Culture and History*, Volume 2. New York: Simon and Schuster Macmillan, 1996.

Moore, Nellie B. "Developing Christian Education in the Local Church" in the *Christian Education Informer*. 51:3. ( December 98—Feb 1999), 21.

Reid, Ira. "The Development of Adult Education for Negroes in the United States," *Journal of Negro Education*. 14:3 (Summer 1945), 200.

Rogers, Alain. "The A.M.E. Church: A Study in Black Nationalism" in *The Black Church*. 1:1 (1975).

Rogers, Donald B. Editor. *Urban Church Education*. Birmingham: Religious Press, 1989.

Schomburg Center for Research in Black Culture. African American Desk Reference. New York: Stonesong Press, Inc. and the New York Public Library, 1999

Shipley, Anthony J. "Choosing and Using Resources in the Black Church." Prepared by the Department of Youth Publications. Nashville: Board of Discipleship of the United Methodist Church. Nashville: Graded Press, 1973.

Smith, Sid. "Historical Perspectives on the Growth Oriented Sunday School," *Black Baptist Sunday School Growth*, compiled by Olivia Cloud. Nashville: Convention Press, 1990.

Smith, Sid. *Reaching the Black Community Through the Sunday School*. Nashville: Convention Press, 1988.

Thomas, Latta. *Biblical Faith and the Black American*. Valley Forge: Judson Press, 1981.

Washington, Booker Taliaferro. *Up From Slavery*. New York: Doubleday and Company, 1971.

Wilmore, Gayraud and James Cone. *Black Theology: A Documentary History,1966-1979*. Maryknoll, New York: Orbis Books, 1979.

Woodson, Carter. *African Background Outlined*. New York: Negro Universities Press, 1936.

Woodson, Carter G. *The Education of the Negro Prior to 1861*. Washington, D.C.: The Association for the Study of Negro Life and History, 1919.

# *General Educational Beliefs in Africa and Historical Highlights of Education in Ancient Egypt*

This chapter will provide the director of Christian education with a general background of education in Africa and a partial history of education in Ancient Egypt. Chapter 2 will allow directors of Christian education to view the seriousness of education in Africa and the many traditions which are part of African Americans' learning patterns. The director will learn how the sources of the African American Sunday school may be traced to the origins of the Sunday School Movement in the dominant church, to the traditions of African education and Ancient Egyptian education (Kemetic education), and to the creativity of African Americans seeking to negotiate an African cultural and religious heritage. The director of Christian education should keep these traditions in mind when planning, making the curriculum contemporary to meet the total needs of African Americans.

Learning about Ancient Egypt will help prepare readers for chapter 7, which will provide insights about the origins of Sunday schools, specifically, the African American Sunday school. In understanding origins of the African American Sunday school, one should understand general educational beliefs in Africa and education in Ancient Egypt, which laid the foundations for the African American Sunday school.

## General Educational Beliefs in Africa

What have been the educational beliefs in Africa? How can these concepts help us understand the shaping of the African American Sunday school? Should the church consider roots of African history when considering the origins of the African American Sunday school? Of course they should. Even though our foreparents were enslaved and dehumanized, many recalled their former life in Africa. Educational practices in Africa help us to understand the idea of education which helped set a foundation for the African American Sunday school.

Today, there are 54 countries in Africa. Sudan is the largest country. Biblically speaking, however, Egypt and Ethiopia are two of the most important locations where Africans resided. In *The African Origin of Civilization: Myth or Reality*? Cheikh Anta Diop states: "Ancient Egypt was a Negro Civilization" (xiv).

In *Egypt: Child of Africa*, Hilliard informs us that "The name *Egypt* is the foreign name given to KMT by the Greeks, nearly two thousand years after the nation was established" (127). Hilliard states that two other names were used for KMT. "In addition to KMT, two other names that natives used were Ta-Mrry (meaning "The Beloved Land" and Tawi meaning "The Two Lands"—Upper and Lower KMT)" (127).

According to an African historical chart of the country of Kemet, the people had a rich development. Kemet periods are divided as follows: Old Kingdom, Dynasties 1-11; Middle Kingdom, Dynasties 11-14; New Kingdom Dynasties 18-24; Late Kingdom, Dynasties 25-30; Greco-Roman Period; Kushite Kingdom; Aksumite/Ethiopian Kingdom; Swahili Trading Cities; Golden Age of West Empires; European Slave Trade; Colonization of Africa.

Dr. Hilliard asserts that some Africans used *The Book of Wise Instruction* for worship. This sacred book with a main focus on Maat and the moral and spiritual obligation for the Maat (Child of Egypt, 126). Maat was also the spirit and method of organizing and conducting the relations of human society. Maat was the moral law of the universe, and embodied truth, justice, righteousness, balance, reciprocity, harmony and order (90). In *Kemet and the African Worldview: Research, Rescue and Restoration*, Maulana Karenga gives another definition for the Maat. He states: "Maat, the quintessential moral and spiritual concept of ancient Kemetic sacred literature, forms the core focus of the instructions..."(92).

Many think that African acceptance of Christianity from European thought was the beginning of religious instruction in Africa. In *Yurugu: An African Centered Critique of European Cultural Thought and Behavior*, Marimba Ani reminds us, "One problem evidenced repeatedly when Europeans look at 'non-Europeans' in what they consider preEuropean cultures is their misunderstanding of the relationship, the one and the many between unity and diversity" (68). One will find that it is not easy to understand a community if one has not lived there.

Before European nations colonized the African continent, Africans were well aware of the importance of education. In *The Maroon Within Us*, Asa Hilliard III provides:

> Long before the colonization of the African continent by European nations, and long before the first-recorded invasions of the African continent by any nation outside the continent, Africans had developed the most sophisticated system of education to be found in early records. Those records show that the African system of education, especially its classical expression in ancient KMT (later called Egypt by the Greeks), was the parent of other systems of education, especially early European education in Greece and Rome (117).

The training for rituals provided much learning. Learned persons were then able to build upon progressing in life. In *Peoples of Africa,* James Gibbs discusses one of the rituals celebrated by peoples of Africa. Many of the rites included religious acts and problem-solving. One example of this is the Jie ritual, which included three main categories: an annual cycle for rainmaking, fertility, and general welfare, all of which contributed to the annual cycle. Prior to the rain season (around early March), a men's initiation would ensure the coming of a new fruitful season. During the early summer, a second tribal ceremony was held to bring and keep the rain (187).

Even Africans in hostile environments experienced ways to improve their education. In *Africa in History,* Basil Davidson remarks on the African community. He provides the insight that Africans mastered their hostile environments by improving their organization and economic understanding, by inventing new tools, and discovering new techniques for living. Communities wanted to maintain a self-confident identity system. It often meant moving from one place to another, beginning a new life and career (52-53). The community teachings help us to understand that education took place in the community, which influenced our religious education and the development of the Sunday school.

This idea leads us to comprehend why much religious education on Sundays, which we now call Sunday school, began in homes. Views from teachers in homes likely led some churches to start a Sunday school.

Africa did not use the term "Sunday school" because religious education took place every day. Likewise, the African American church should allow for teaching during the week, whether it is school or ministry meetings. Teaching must go beyond the Sunday church school and Bible studies.

African Americans can then conclude that religious ideas originated in Africa. These ideas set the foundation for the African American Sunday school. Africans arrived in America recalling older traditions. Many blacks still praise God according to African traditions, and even though in prior years blacks were taught to read the Bible that whites provided, learning Scripture in America was not a strange idea for African Americans. They could readily recite and interpret much Scripture that they were self-taught or taught on Sundays in homes (what we call Sunday school). Based on African educational practices prior to use of a church building, African Americans knew about Sunday school. As a matter of fact, before the church building plan or the blueprint for the Sunday school was proposed, African Americans had long been a part of the Sunday school classroom.

## History of Education in Ancient Egypt

Does religious education have roots in Africa? If such roots exist, should they be considered the backbone for the Sunday school? Should these efforts be considered a part of African Americans' roots? The answer to all of these questions is yes. Many view the Cushites of Egypt as founders of religious education. The Kemetics, heirs of the Cushites in Ancient Egypt, are the most documented source for our study. Egyptians have always given much regard to their education.

Kemet was Ancient Egypt in North Africa. Kemet was conquered, but near the Euphrates River, near Kush. Kemet, which is not in existence today, was part of what we know today as the Nubia/Kush region, adjacent to the Nile River from the sixth cataract to South of the first cataract. This area of the Nile, called Nubian Corridor, linked Kemet with Central and East Africa. The Nile River Valley was settled by Africans about 18,000 BCE. Africans came from the Mountains of the Moon, the Blue Nile, and the Sahara Region.

Kemet was the beginning of African civilization. In *The Maroon Within Us*, Dr. Asa Hilliard III states that Europeans were not the first group to conquer Kemet. "Ancient KMT was conquered first by Asians, later by Europeans, and finally by an Arabic-Asian population" (124). In *Kemet and the African Worldview: Research, Rescue and Restoration*, Hilliard states: "The highest aim of Egyptian education was for one to become godlike through the revelation of one's own "Neter" of how God is revealed in the person" (144). Their first aim in education was to make a personal decision in life. Hilliard adds: "The lower education system, no matter how unstructured, allowed for a natural progress along a path that reached certain points... a learner could reach the major choice of his or her life" (144).

Hilliard also informs us that the educational system in Ancient Egypt gave attention to character development. The method was a collective effort. "Teachers" or "Masters" modeled the behavior that they expected the initiates to learn (142-43). These facts help us understand Ancient Egypt and her original name, Kemet. In *Kemet and the African Worldview*, Jacob H. Carruthers states: " The people called themselves Kemites, the Black ones" (3).

Hilliard further comments on the Kemetics: "While the population of KMT was somewhat ethnically and racially mixed, even in the early kingdoms, it was southern Black African leadership that founded KMT and governed it during its golden ages" (118). Hilliard discusses the operating framework for the KMT. "KMT was a Black African nation during its most important development periods" (119). Hilliard informs: "Ancient KMT was a high tech society. It required armies of educated people. The first step in the formal process of general education was training as a scribe, which was a highly honored profession. The route to sacred or secular office was through the scribal school" (122).

The historian also notes: "Kemetic education can be described as 'functional' a blend of theory and practice, a 'holistic' education" (124). Kemetics did not simply educate their own, but many abroad also observed their educational techniques. Hilliard comments:

> Kemetic education is our best window to ancient African education continent wide. Kemetic education is the parent of 'western' education, and therefore it must be understood if ancient and modern western education are to be understood. Kemetic education is a system that can and, in my opinion, should provide guidance for the organization of the education of our people today. (126)

Kemetic education was unique because the Kemetics had their own texts. Maulana Karenga states that Kemetics had black sacred texts (84). There was not a certain Kemetic sacred text, but written examples were used. Dr. Carruthers cites beginning efforts to restore the Kemetic sacred text in the form of the *Husia* (85). According to Karenga, the structure of the *Husia* includes sections such as The Book of Knowing the Creations, The Book of Prayers and Sacred Praises, The Books of the Moral Narrative, The Books of Wise Instruction, The Books of Contemplation, The Book of Declarations of Virtues, and The Books of Rising Like Ra (87-88).

In *Her-Bak: The Living Face of Ancient Egypt*, Isha Schwaller De Lubicz provides helpful information about teaching in Ancient Egypt. Teaching methods varied in Ancient Egypt. The laws of Maat (consciousness and truth) were applied.

The authors provide this information in their documentary appendix. They transmitted their knowledge in several ways:

a) By training man's senses and mind...the laws of Maat, which means the conformity of the name of each thing with its true nature....

b) By inducing people to "follow the lesson of Thot and Seshat," the Neters of writing, of the geometrical patterns and shapes occurring in nature, and all configurations and signatures,... reveal its character and properties.

c) By developing in the reader the unifying vision, by superimposition of the various aspects (physical, spiritual, historical) of a subject in one and the same text or picture. This was the spirit in which they taught sciences... Ancient Egypt always saw the cause through the effect... the essential characteristics of the Egyptian method: observation of the concrete fact or the concrete symbol of a fact, for the purpose of rousing in the student the evocation of its abstract aspect (325-326).

*Her-Bak: The Living Face of Ancient Egypt* discusses ancient African teaching materials and subjects. Teachers used materials that consisted of inscriptions engraved in the temples, steles and statues, papyri and ostraca, and inscriptions in tombs and on sarcophagi. They taught philosophy, schoolboy exercises and secular letters. The subjects also included: "Cosmogonical myths, astronomical inscriptions, hymns and poems with initiatory meaning, philosophical narratives, historical records—almost always symbolic ..." (322 ). Most of the mentioned materials are in books such as *Book of the Dead, Book of Day and Night, Book of Breathing and Book of Amenhotep Son of Hapu, Litanies of Sokaris, Book of Passage Through Eternity, and Litanies of the Sun.* The authors state that there existed two classes of schools, a primary school for social concerns and the temple which taught higher concerns (323).

*Her-Bak* also provides information about student writing tools. In Ancient Egypt, the student used various writing tools, one of which was the palette. "The palette was a long, narrow, rectangular wooden tablet, with a container for the reeds and two sockets for cakes of black and red ink. The scribe wrote on papyrus, tablets of stuccoed wood, shards, pottery fragments, or limestone splinters (ostraca)" (333).

Ancient Egypt, like any other nation, had religious beliefs. The book *Her-Bak* helps us understand some of their views. According to Hilliard, religiously, Ancient Egypt held that there were three worlds: Heaven, Earth and Dwat (the transition between the abstract world of the causal Powers and the concrete world of phenomena or world of nature) (340). Some of these beliefs were embedded in our ancestors and passed on to many slaves. We find similar beliefs among Christians today, as Christians believe in heaven and hell.

As we study and learn more about Kemetics, one can find that African Americans have a rich background in educational practices. The desire for education in Africa has led African Americans to seek education in both religious and secular forms. The African American Sunday school has learned much from Kemetic views.

## SOURCES CITED FOR GENERAL EDUCATION
## IN AFRICA

Azevedo, Mario, editor. *Africana Studies— A Survey of Africa and the African Diaspora*. Durham: Carolina Academic Press, 1993.

Carruthers, Jacob H. "The Wisdom of Governance in Kemet." in *Kemet and the African Worldview—Research, Rescue, and Restoration*. Los Angeles: University of Sankore Press, 1986.

Davidson, Basil. *Africa in History*. New York: Collier Books, 1974.

Diop, Cheikh Anta. *The African Origin of Civilization*. Mercer Cook, Editor. Chicago: Lawrence Hill Books, 1974.

Gibbs, James L. Jr. editor. *Peoples of Africa*. Chicago: Holt, Rinehart and Winston Inc., 1965.

Hilliard, Asa III. *Egypt: Child of Africa*, edited by Ivan Van Sertima. New Brunswick: Transactional Publishers, 1995.

Hilliard, Asa III. *The Maroon Within Us*. Baltimore: Black Classic Press, 1995.

Karenga, Maulana. "Restoration of the Husia: Reviving a Sacred Legacy" in *Kemet and the African Worldview: Research, Rescue and Restoration*. Los Angeles: University of Sankore Press, 1986.

Lubicz, Isha De Schwalller. *Her-Bak—The Living Face of Ancient Egypt*. New York: Inner Traditions International LTD, 1978.

Marimba Ani. *Yurugu: An African Centered Critique of European Cultural Thought and Behavior*. Trenton, New Jersey: African World Press Inc., 1994.

## SOURCES CITED FOR KEMETIC EDUCATION

A Historical Chart: Africa-A Historical Chronology.

Lubicz, Isha De Schwaller. *HER-BAK—The Living Face of Ancient Egypt*. New York: Inner Traditions International, 1978.

Hilliard, Asa III. "Kemetics Concepts in Education" in *Egypt Child of Africa* edited by Ivan Van Sertima. New Brunswick: Transaction Publishers, 1994.

Karenga, Maulana and Jacob H. Carruthers. *Kemet and the African Worldview-Research, Rescue and Restoration*. Los Angeles: University of Sankore Press, 1986.

# CHAPTER 3

# The DCE (Director of Christian Education)

This chapter is written to remind the director of Christian education of the major role that the director must play. In this chapter, one will find some definitions for the term *Director of Christian Education,* help the DCE prepare for initial questions, (if seeking a job, or assisting other directors in the job search), discuss some things to look for in a contract, and lastly, provide some considerations for the DCE on the job.

## Who Is the Director of Education?

Who is the director of Christian education? The director of Christian education is the person in charge of the entire Christian educational program. The director is the ex-officio for all meetings. He or she should monitor all Christian education. The director of Christian education is the backbone of all educational processes to be implemented in the church. In *How to Develop a Department of Christian Education within the Local Baptist Church,* Alvin Bernstine provides one definition: "The director is the person who, in a very real sense, gives shape to the educational mentality of the congregation" (64).

Some churches call the director of Christian education, the minister of education. Other churches may choose a leader, such as a deacon or superintendent. Churches with memberships of 300 and over should have a full-time Director of Christian Education. Smaller churches should also consider a full-time director, but in all cases, at least a part-time director. This book will use the term *Director of Christian Education.* The term will be abbreviated DCE.

Many times the DCE is overlooked in the establishment of the Christian education program. Without the DCE or a leader for the department, the Christian education program would be indescribable. In addition, a director without a sound Christian education program serves little purpose for maintaining his or her title.

The director of Christian education is responsible for all education in the church. The DCE must prepare people for serving. He or she must know the job. The job description will help the director to understand his or her role.

The DCE should discuss all contractual terms with the employer. The length of contract and termination of the position or employee should be mutually understood. If the position is terminated because the church wants to do something else, reasonable severance (enough months notice for the DCE to seek a new professional position), relocation fees, and prorated benefits should be rendered. Some churches add responsibilities to the DCE's agenda such as giving eulogies for funerals, visiting the sick, preaching more than once a month, requiring the DCE to sit in the pulpit each Sunday, and participate in performing marriages.

It takes more than forty hours a week to guide Christian education. Most secular jobs require set hours, but the DCE should be flexible as to work days, evenings, nights, and weekends because many leaders in the church work during the day. The DCE must not get locked into a 9-5 schedule plus added times and responsibilities, unless this is agreed upon with compensation. Overtime may be substituted for normal hours.

## Questions the Director of Christian Education May Ask an Employer

As I sat on Amtrak, March 31, 1998, headed for an interview to discuss a possible vacancy in Christian education (to be conducted before several groups in a large rented room on a university campus), I quickly had to reflect on the questions that I needed to ask the committee. I recommend including the following thirty questions:

1. Ask the committee what their vision is for the church and its ministry.
2. What are their teaching and learning goals for youth and children and other age groups?
3. What special challenges do they face in making an attempt to reach these goals?

4. What are the strengths and weaknesses of your educational ministry?
5. What expectations do you have of a director of Christian education?
6. Has the educational ministry been involved in missions and vocational interest?
7. Does the DCE have an option to suggest a new curriculum?
8. Is there a listing for ministries under the Board of Christian Education?
9. Will a budget be included for attending workshops or conferences, to buy professional books, to buy DCE recommended awards/recognitions for departmental workers? What is the church policy for awards, i.e., plaques? Will funds be available for local job-related travel expenses, for professional books, and for meetings with special invited guests?
10. Will an assistant or intern assist me?
11. Will a secretary assist me?
12. Is the director required to be a member of the church?
13. What is the church guideline for fund-raising? What about children/youth fund raising?
14. Is a church handbook available? Is there a handbook for the department of Christian education? When were they last revised? Will the director be responsible for revising the handbooks?
15. Is there a youth and/or children's church? Will I be responsible for this leadership or will the pastor assume this task?
16. What supervisor do I report to and how often?
17. If problems arise in the ministries, are leaders allowed to intervene before I am given opportunity to rectify matters? (The DCE should attempt to resolve problems in ministries before others are informed.)
18. Is there a Board of Christian Education? If so, what is its purpose? Am I allowed to reconstruct the board's policies and to make recommendations for leadership and set agenda for meetings? Will the chair report to me? (The chair should report to the DCE and the DCE reports to the pastor/church.)
19. Am I required to attend conferences and/or council meetings? (I find that it is best to send leaders to this meeting so that the DCE can stay free from as many meetings as possible.)

20. Are there supervisors for ministries? What are their roles? In the case of deacons, is there a deacon who provides spiritual advice to leaders? (The important key is that deacons understand that a supervisor provides spiritual leadership. Make sure also that leaders follow church guidelines, not those of institute or direct program development.)
21. What is the procedure to add a new ministry under Christian education?
22. Do I have the right to interview, make selections, and deploy the Christian education staff?
23. May I begin this position with three to six months of observation/planning before implementation?
24. Is there a director of administration?
25. Is there a Christian education budget? Are budgetary guidelines established?
26. Does the employer provide insurance for my personal books, folders and liability coverages?
27. Will the pastor approve all speakers, preachers and workshop leaders or will the director assist in this duty?
28. Will overtime be provided for hours worked beyond the regular forty hours? Will overtime be provided for preaching, attending programs and events?
29. Once employed, will I find that I should have read the contract for tricky words, i.e., to "assist" rather than "lead" the Christian education team?
30. Will all details about salary, vacation, retirement, housing and the entire financial package be a part of the contract?
    Asking the questions will enlighten the employer about your knowledge of some possible misunderstandings between the employer and the DCE. These questions/answers will hopefully create an interest in the employer to rethink current "terms" for hiring. The DCE is similar to the pastor/preacher—If he or she is worthy of hire, then "pay" for his or her services.

## Some Counsel to the DCE in the African American Church

How many times have I said, "Lord, where can I get help in determining basics for guiding a Christian education program?" Sometimes the little things cost me many days of frustration, pain, anger, and almost gave me a desire to give up. One cannot take for granted that other members of your team will provide you with answers; although these members are helpful, oftentimes they too do not have answers to our questions. My final word to the DCE is fourfold as follows:

## A. Be Aware of Adversaries

The DCE will likely face adversaries. Many adversaries will greet the DCE in Christ, but usually they can be detected by other behaviors. Adversaries are both quiet and loquacious. They walk into the DCE's office making demands. They want to know what the DCE is about. There are those who look like sheep but are wolves in sheep's clothing. Some adversaries are in face-to-face agreement, but in closed meetings are against the DCE and the program.

## B. Watch and Pray

Scripture teaches us to watch and pray. Watching and praying is a way to observe behavior and then take concerns to God in prayer. The DCE should observe what goes on in Christian education. At the same time, the DCE should pray as well. Prayer is one way to thank God for blessings and to ask Him for guidance. The DCE might find that the Christian education program seems to be at a standstill.

In such cases, watch and pray. God has a way to provide insights to help solve our problems. Consider reading Scriptures about watching and praying. Luke 21:36 and Matthew 26:41 tell us the following:

"Watch out and keep praying that you can escape all that is going to happen and that the Son of Man will be pleased with you" (Luke 21:36).

"Stay awake and pray that you won't be tested. You want to do what is right, but you are weak" (Matthew 26:41).

## C. Check Your Attitude

The DCE should maintain a spirit-filled attitude. The DCE must maintain a kind, congenial spirit. This is by no means to say, "Let people take advantage of you." When trouble comes, the Holy Spirit is available to intervene for you. The DCE, other leaders in the church, and leaders in Christian education must work as a team. No one person owns the enterprise. Leadership is understood when the DCE and leaders recognize that they are all servants. We must flee from and avoid the "I- Centered" mentality.

## D. Consider These Nine Points

The following suggested nine points will help the DCE become acquainted with the department and its workers. **The DCE should:**

### 1. Know the Constitution or By-Laws

The DCE should first see if a constitution is available. Many African American churches still neglect to have a constitution because of their roots in oral tradition. If the DCE does not find a written constitution, the DCE should quickly suggest and guide the church to develop a constitution. A written constitution is preferred. Sometimes the pastor may ask a committee to revise the constitution; the DCE is then usually a reader of the final product. The DCE is not employed to develop new laws, but often the DCE's assistance is requested. The church has existed years before the DCE and will continue to exist years after the DCE. Knowing what is or is not acceptable is a good beginning for any DCE. The constitution is by-laws or guides for what should or should not be done and consequences for violations.

### 2. Know Your Supervisor

Many churches attempt to allow the entire congregation to supervise the DCE. If the DCE is not careful, deacons, trustees, and parishioners will all instruct you how to do certain things. It is better to report to one person. When problems arise, go to *your supervisor*. The supervisor is usually the pastor.

### 3. Maintenance, Space Requests and the Church Calendar

There will be times when something will go wrong in your office, in a classroom, or general set-up is needed (for example, set-up for a workshop). Having a good rapport with the maintenance supervisor is very important in such cases. Just as important is to know who is in charge of space requests. Some churches have a secretary to assist. When space is needed for a meeting, event or workshop, it is wise to know where to seek assistance.

## 4. Know the People You Talk To

It is important to know persons who can assist the DCE. Often-times, knowing that person in the congregation who is willing to pray with and for the DCE makes a big difference. The DCE can usually detect helpful individuals. Those who are really concerned will pray and cry with the DCE. The DCE should never feel that he or she can develop the program alone. Sometimes co-workers can remind us of simple things that we have overlooked. Avoid those who gossip or who cannot keep church business confidential.

## 5. Food Events for Ministries

Many churches survive economically on tithes and offerings alone, which is preferred. Events involving food require serious thought. Learn what ministries are given the privilege of having dinners at the church's expense, and to what extent. Many ministry leaders call a meal "refreshments." If refreshments are allowed, "How much?" is the question. Do not allow leaders to burden you with their new rules or commands, when in fact they never were allowed to have food for events in past years. New suggestions should be thought through care-fully before suggesting change to by-laws.

## 6. Food/Refreshments Requests

The DCE should know to whom he or she should submit food or refreshment requests. Be familiar with the required advance notice and the details required. After submitting the request, make sure that you get a response, approval or disapproval. Unattended food and re-freshment requests can become a disturbing moment for the DCE, department leaders, ministry leaders, and ministry participants. In other words, if attendees are awaiting food, and there is none, attendees will likely get upset.

## 7. Deadlines

The DCE should know the church's deadline for turning in the annual budget and department calendar. The department ministry leader should turn in both of these items to the DCE at a specified date. The DCE should turn in budgets and calendars for review to the proper persons or committees. The DCE should attend the annual calendar-planning meeting. The same concerns should exist for completing the annual calendar for the department.

## 8. Procedures

The DCE should understand the procedures for ordering supplies as early as possible. Ordering supplies can become a problem that the DCE does not need. When certain materials are needed for the office, such as typing ribbons and paper, you should have a supply on hand. It is best to store your own supplies. Many times when items are needed, finding the person or disturbing a person can pose problems which might interrupt one's day. As simple a thing as not getting a stamp can ruin one's entire day. A busy person in charge of stamps, unwilling to stop his or her own work, could delay the work of the DCE. Some people in charge feel they need to determine when supplies are disbursed. Procedures for duplicating materials or printing requests, availability of the fax machine, where faxes are placed, how they are collected, and having access to the room where the fax is stored should be known. It is far better to have a fax and copier for the department. Procedures for receiving mail should also be known: who puts up mail and at what time, who receives special C.O.D.'s and signature required mail, and how to receive and mail parcels. The DCE should know the budget amounts and how to make the requests.

## 9. Know What Goes on in Ministries

The DCE should know what goes on in all ministries. Time management is important for tracking this knowledge. Ministry leaders should be responsible for their department. All ministry leaders are required to submit reports to their department leader concerning their ministry events. Reports should include what took place during the last few months, and the present month, and what is anticipated in the next few months. In addition, approvals for program bulletins, advertisement flyers and ministry events, are given to the department director, who in turn informs the DCE. The DCE then informs the pastor.

**WORK CITED**

Bernstine, Alvin. *How to Develop a Department of Christian Education Within the Local Church.* Nashville: Townsend Press, 1995.

# CHAPTER 4

# Suggested Lists
# for the Director
# of Christian Education

The DCE may find that lists will help in organizing or reorganizing the Christian education program, for even the trained DCE may forget "simple" things. I often find myself "pondering" what should be done next. This chapter will enlighten or remind the DCE about various administrative concerns. Three lists will be suggested: Twelve things for the DCE to glance at: seven things the DCE should be cautious about in Christian education leadership, and the ABC's of ways to organize the DCE's plans.

**LIST ONE**: *Twelve Things the DCE Should Be Aware of When Working in Christian Education in the Local Church:*

## 1. Tradition

The African American church is known for her tradition, since tradition is very important. However, many members think tradition allows them to own the church and its ministry. Traditional views should not prevent positive change. Of course, the DCE should not attempt to change everything overnight. At the same time, though, the DCE must not allow tradition to impede the progress of Christian education. Tradition should never hinder the DCE from suggesting new ways for doing Christian education.

The church knows that tradition is important. It is harmful for anyone to attempt to rob the church of its tradition. Thus, all changes should be made gradually in order to update the church.

While the DCE should value tradition, he or she should also be free to suggest that the church allow today's society to interpret and refine traditional views.

Traditional thinking has caused many parishioners to feel that they

45

own certain areas in the church. It may be one brick, one pew, or one window that a parishioner has donated to the church. But making donations to the church does not equate investment in church property. In addition, many think that they own the ministries in which they serve. God alone is the Head of Christian ministries. We are only servants. Leaders sometimes close doors to others because they simply want to own the ministry and keep their select group in the ministry circle.

Change is very important. The church cannot afford to allow tradition to block the progress of the church. (For example, many teachers and leaders have taught and led for twenty or fifty years.) Things do change, and leaders and teachers must also be willing to change as well in order to meet the needs of today's congregation.

## 2. Curriculum

The DCE may not agree with the total curriculum. The curriculum belongs to the entire community. But again, a curriculum should not be modified overnight. The change must take place over a period of time. The curriculum should be modified only after it is used and tested. All leaders should be a part of the planning process. This section will be further discussed in the next chapter.

## 3. Ownership of Ministries

Many ministry leaders have been leaders for years. Some of these leaders might feel threatened if you instruct them in how to lead ministries. Leaders must be taught that ministries are owned by God and that leaders are only agents for God's work to be completed. The DCE must suggest training programs to enlighten leaders about Christian education. The DCE should suggest removal of all disruptive leaders to the pastor. This should only be done after the DCE has followed procedures for conferences and provided the required church warnings, except in extenuating circumstances. The DCE should not attempt to remove leadership but to show leaders how to improve their skills. Many leaders will remain in leadership positions until the end of their tenure or death.

## 4. Meetings

The DCE is faced with many meetings. It is most important to attend those meetings related to enhancing the work of ministries. Meetings are best held with smaller numbers, rather than with a large group. Meetings with individual leaders usually work best. As a rule, try to limit attending numerous meetings. Usually, a telephone conference can replace some meetings. The DCE must keep in mind that most of the workers are volunteers and they should not be required to attend all meetings.

## 5. Activities for Ministries

Everyone likes extracurricular activities. Such activities are needed in the church, but should be carefully planned. An activity without a purpose is of questionable meaning. Some ministries have too many "fun" activities per year. These include a number of retreats, field trips and excursions that often result in a misuse of God's money. Ministries need to limit fun activities. How much is too much? For example, some youth groups misuse funds by going on many field trips or retreats per year. If there is no recreation department, ministry leaders should schedule fun activities. These "fun" activities should be included in your program and be planned by the entire department. Learning activities must supercede "fun activities." Fun activities are great, but learning activities, those activities related to the subject, are suggested instead. These kinds of activities help students learn the subject studied.

## 6. Bad Attitudes

The DCE should carefully watch for various inappropriate attitudes around the church. Many people have an un-Christianlike attitude. Many Christians treat each other worse than sinners do. Christians often forget how to be meek and humble (see Galatians 5:22). Some Christians desire to be only leaders and not followers. Some followers attempt to instruct leaders. For example, the DCE should be in charge of suggesting changes or additions to a program. Oftentimes, however, followers will not hear what God is saying through the director because the followers are doing all the suggesting.

The DCE may hear God through others, but others should not dictate how the DCE will carry out what God has instructed.

The African American church must teach people why Christians need to cultivate a good attitude. Some members with bad attitudes bring their home problems to the church. They in turn use the Christian education program as a dumping ground for problems. One must never allow the bad attitudes to get in the way of the progress of the program.

## 7. The Board of Christian Education

The board should be seen as a helpful extension to the Christian education department. The DCE should not spend all of his or her time worrying about the board meetings. Limit the number of board meetings to every other month or quarter. The chair or dean of the Board of Christian Education may conduct meetings. The DCE should review and approve the agenda, preferably two weeks prior to the actual board meeting. The organization of a board will be discussed in the next chapter.

## 8. The Board of Deacons

Meetings with the deacons can be the best or the worst thing to happen to the DCE. Deacons are most helpful when they discuss needs for leaders and ministries. They are least helpful when they attempt to lead the Christian educational program, especially when they insert archaic views based on past church or personal experiences. Some churches allow deacons and trustees to act as "pastors," which creates a problem for the DCE. If the deacons attempt to serve as pastors, they each could request the DCE to provide reports. Deacons should not receive DCE reports. The pastor receives such reports. The pastor may include the DCE's report as an agenda item for any deacon board meeting.

It is better to schedule meetings with the chairman of the Deacon Board, or the entire Deacon Board per the pastor's recommendation, than to meet with the entire Deacon Board. It is even better when the pastor will share the DCE report with the deacons.

## 9. Programs and Services

The DCE must never feel obligated to attend every ministry program and service. The DCE can take on too much responsibility. Making too many commitments to appear on a program can be harmful and exhausting. It is nice for the DCE to be seen, but the work of the DCE is not for show. The DCE should attend programs and services, but he or she does not have to attend every one.

Some DCEs attend programs and services in order to preach, if they are licensed to do so. Preaching is a great and much-needed skill, but still the DCE should recall that the responsibility of the DCE is leading a department, not preaching. Preaching schedules should be developed on personal time and at the request of the pastor.

## 10. Budgetary Concerns

It is important for the DCE to avoid budgetary complaints. Some department leaders and ministry leaders attempt to take all problems to the DCE. The DCE must determine carefully when to respond to a ministry leader's needs. The finance department is in charge of the budget and other church finances. Even when things do not seem in order, the finance team is held responsible for all finance procedures and actions. Most financial complaints or concerns should thus be addressed to the secretary of finance.

The DCE should encourage leaders to adhere to financial guidelines. The DCE must see that ministries do not exceed their budgets.

## 11. Confidentiality

Confidentiality is very important in church work. The job of the DCE is to assure such confidentiality. Ministry leaders should understand the urgency for confidentiality. When leaders cannot confide in the DCE, ministry often becomes unimportant. Sometimes students will discuss personal matters with their ministry leaders. Students may lose confidence in the DCE or ministry leader if confidentiality is not provided. The DCE must see that church law and confidentiality are taught to leaders.

## 12. Selecting Ministry Leaders and Workers

Selecting ministry leaders and workers is a major job of the DCE. It is not easy to select a good team. The DCE should recommend paid positions for ministry leaders whenever possible. When they are paid, leaders will be more likely to report on time and to complete their assignments. When the leaders are volunteers, they should be assigned to a position because the Holy Spirit has directed the DCE to discover talents and gifts in these volunteers that match their job descriptions.

Board members should be allowed to submit names to the board's chair to fill vacant positions. The DCE may allow the chair of the Board of Christian Education to submit two names for each vacant board position or have board members vote by ballot and the top two names for each vacant position is referred to the DCE; the DCE should then make final recommendations to the pastor. In some cases, the pastor may allow the DCE to make final recommendations for filling board vacancies. In most cases, the church or the Board of Deacons introduces all leadership appointments to the congregation, which in turn requires leaders to be formally installed, usually at the beginning of each church calendar year. It is better not to advertise for leaders and workers because many people may be rejected and become disappointed with the department, and could leave the church because of being rejected. Some individuals have proper qualifications, but one may find that often the most qualified may not serve the church very well. The church should seek individuals who will build up the church (1 Corinthians 14:12).

**LIST TWO:** *Seven Things the DCE Should be Cautious About in Christian Education Leadership:*

1. Accepting last-minute invitations.
2. Previewing literature and materials that require future purchases. Be sure to acquire a "bio"of the author. Checking references may be wise.
3. Receiving deals or discounts that sound appealing, but require advance payment for products, goods and services.
4. Members who always praise you or your work.
5. Dinners or luncheons to discuss your work.
6. Helpers who volunteer to aid in ministry preparations, such as plays, costumes, arts and crafts, but who will not adhere to deadlines.

7. Videotaping and taping interviews without knowledge of the purpose and ownership of master tapes.

**LIST THREE:** *Suggested Ways to Help with Administration*

So many times, the DCE may ask the question, "What are some things that should be considered the first few months on the job?" The following suggestions are only a starting point for the DCE. The order may or may not be the same for your administration.

## 1. Get a Large Desk Calendar for the Year

Keep all appointments and dates on the calendar. Many directors and leaders in Christian education do not respond to telephone calls and do not correspond with letters or memos, and so often the work of Christian education seems poorly done. The DCE should respond to all communications. Make sure you give a good example in this area. Many leaders in mega churches as well as small ones do not seem to care about communications, which shows poor organizational skills. The DCE will be respected for good organizational skills. Keeping a desk calendar is the first organizational step for a DCE.

## 2. Organize Your Office

It is very important to have a neat and organized office. The first impression is usually one that will last. Visitors will question a messy or junky office. They will often relate the looks of the office to the work of the DCE. Many offices look like a tornado just came through. The office of a leader tells one a lot about that person. Leaders will often say, "Excuse my office." One excuses the office, but not the person. At times, we all will have days when things are unorganized, but being unorganized should not last for weeks.

The office should have some nice designer touches, such as colorful paintings and displayed educational materials to show a sign of education. The DCE's books and certificates may or may not be in the office; this is a matter of preference.

## 3. Organize Your File Cabinets

The DCE needs two or more file cabinets in the office. The files should include labeled folders. Labels may differ from these suggested ones because of your own personal needs. The following may be suggested: Budgets; calendar; catalogs; church history; church mission; church handbook; clerical forms; correspondence received; correspondence sent; correspondence to chair of the Christian Education Board; correspondence to pastor; correspondence to and from the Sunday church school, including teachers and superintendent; correspondence from ministry leaders; counseling sessions; conventions; denominational materials; Deacon Board roster; fire roster; forms for ministry leaders; important numbers for church leaders (for example, deacons and trustees); job descriptions; letterheads; maintenance forms; ministry reports; observations of church school; leaders; ministries; suggestions; surveys; tax-exempt number; Trustee Board roster; financial committee; requisition copies for food; requisition copies for space; requisitions copies for funds, and workshops.

## 4. Look at the Environment

Go through the church and look at the entire environment. Look for pictures and posters. Notice how things are posted: Look at bulletin boards and their appearance; classrooms space, decorations in classrooms; teaching supplies; locations and general rooms for meetings; the entire educational area, offices, tables, carpet and floors. All of these give a broad picture of the church. Make notes of your observations. After observing, make suggestions for improvement. Share the written report with the pastor. Do not imply that you are changing anything, make only suggestions. There may be as many as thirty pages of observations and recommendations. Many things will be added as time goes on. It may take years for some things to be corrected and for some leaders to consider some recommendations. The key is to remind the pastor and leaders about needs in Christian education.

## 5. Request Mission Statement for the Church from Pastor

Some pastors may not know what a mission statement is. A mission statement is a document that tells where the church is headed. It may or may not include denominational views. Some churches are affiliated with denominations and conventions, but are self-governing in by-laws. Some mission statements include the church's and pastor's views for the future of the church. Any preacher called to serve should eventually have his or her vision as a part of the mission statement. If the pastor does not have a vision, the people will perish.

## 6. Look at the Flow Chart for the Church

The church should have a flow chart that shows the hierarchy of leadership positions. The director of Christian education may assist the pastor in developing this flow chart. This flow chart will inform the church and its visitors of the order of command. The church flow chart should be placed in a visible area of the church, usually the narthex (what some incorrectly call the vestibule, a secular area in the Jerusalem temple). The Christian educational chart should be placed in an area where Christian education takes place. A flow chart will be discussed in the next chapter.

## 7. Request Names, Addresses and Contacts of All Leaders

Make sure you have a list of names, phone numbers, and addresses for the following church leaders: pastor, ministerial staff, deacons, deaconesses, trustees, directors, department leaders, Christian Education Board members, all ministry leaders in Christian education as well as other areas, all workers who are part of each ministry in Christian education and Sunday church school superintendents, departmental leaders, Sunday school teachers and substitutes, and other leaders (Ask the general superintendent to submit this information).

## 8. Learn Financial Procedures
  a. Know all financial guidelines for your department.
  b. Know the guidelines for signing requisitions (requests).
  c. Inform ministry leaders of guidelines and your responsibilities.
  d. Inform leaders about steps to request funds.
  e. Leaders should be informed about all deadlines.
  f. The DCE should have an understanding of financial reports that will list current ministry balances.
  g. Copies of every submission should be kept by the ministry leader and the DCE. The approval for funds should be announced by the finance team. It is also wise for the finance team to contact the DCE for denied requests.
  h. The DCE must understand procedures for food and general ministry requests. Some churches prefer ministries to have

a separate budget for food requests, while other churches supply refreshments and must approve major food requests.

i. Some churches request that the DCE be the last one to sign and approve ministry requisitions. Clearly comprehend your responsibilities and limitations.

## 9. Obtain a Sunday Church School Calendar and Schedule of Classes and Their Locations.

A schedule of all classes, teachers, room numbers and locations should be a part of the DCE's records. A schedule of classes is usually made up by the DCE. The superintendent implements the DCE's suggestions. If you are newly hired, you may have to ask the superintendent for this information. In large churches, the DCE may appoint and train other leaders to assist with responsibilities in Christian education. As DCE, observe Sunday school classes, paying attention to both teachers and students, and to leaders in the Sunday church school. Pay attention to teaching styles, course content, and how students are motivated to accept the content being taught. Also notice the location of classes. For example, elderly persons often cannot climb steps and should not be asked to meet on an upper floor. Children should be kept on first floors and away from the main sanctuary. The Sunday church school calendar is also very important. It should include the opening school year date, graduation date, Christmas events, VBS dates, and dates of all other Sunday church school events.

## 10. Request Calendars from all Christian Education Ministry Leaders.

It is very important that the director and pastor know everything that goes on in ministries. A calendar will remind the DCE about events and activities that go on in the various ministries.

## 11. Look at Curriculum for the Sunday Church School and All Ministries Under Christian Education

Examine whatever material leaders are using to teach the Word of God: versions of the Bible, printed literature in the curriculum, and supplementary literature. Develop a committee to evaluate Sunday church school literature. Usually, evaluation should take place six months to one year from the revised or new DCE tenure. See Dr. Oneal Sandidge's *Teacher Training in the African American Church* as one source for suggestions in evaluating Sunday church school literature. The next chapter will provide insights on developing the curriculum.

## 12. Look at All Audiovisual Equipment

It is important to have a person in charge of distributing and loaning equipment. The DCE and the person in charge for distributing equipment should maintain an inventory list. The director is responsible for ordering and repairing equipment. Equipment may include: a VCR, a television, flip charts, recorders, and an overhead projector. It is better to store equipment for Christian education in a separate area from general church equipment. The DCE and the Department of Christian Education may find distributing equipment for the church-at-large and the department to be too big of a task.

## 13. Visit All Ministries

It is important to occasionally visit all ministries. Develop a letter to introduce yourself to department and ministry leaders. The DCE should spend time to meet with department and ministry leaders to learn about the ministries under Christian education. The DCE should make sure that leaders understand their assignments and the work of the ministry. The DCE will assist leaders in program development. The DCE should have a checklist when observing ministries.

When visiting ministries, be open-minded. Do not be concerned about gossip. It is best to believe that all leaders can be the best leaders. We all have faults and make mistakes. Forget what happened under the leadership of the previous director. The DCE may develop survey questions to learn more about leaders. File information on your visits. Study the ministry's activities and its annual calendar. Then do not forget to survey the congregation and participants in the ministry to learn ministry needs.

## 14. Visit the Sunday Church School

Visiting the Sunday school is very important for the director. Sit in on classes to observe teachers, content taught, student behavior, and student needs. Also spend time to make suggestions to leaders to improve the Sunday school and develop new training ideas for the Sunday school.

## 15. Meet with Ministry Leaders

During the beginning of the DCE's term, the DCE should get to know department and ministry leaders, and in some cases, directors and other workers in the Department of Christian Education. The DCE is responsible for all activities, programs, and ministry events. This includes reviewing tapes and videos before leaders show them to ministries. Afrocentric characters is an important component of media viewed in the African American church; however, videos with African American characters may or may not meet the needs of a given church. The content is most important.

Suggestions for improving ministries are very much needed. The DCE must not exercise the given authority in such a way to intimidate others. Make others feel a part of the plan. It is better to say "I suggest" than "we will do." When leaders are a part of the team, leaders will usually work with the DCE. The DCE should be careful with words.

## 16. Meet with the Sunday Church School Leaders

The general superintendent is the person responsible for the Sunday church school. He or she reports to the DCE. There are times when the DCE should meet with all leaders of the Sunday church school: The general superintendent, assistant superintendents, departmental superintendents, teachers, and other Sunday church school workers. Other times, the superintendent can inform the DCE.

## 17. Work at Training Leaders

Training is very important for ministry leaders. Training for teachers is also needed: new or prospective teachers and in-services for present teachers. The following suggested workshops may be helpful in considering training your ministry leaders such as: "Development of Christian character"; "How to deal with various attitudes"; "How to understand development of the life cycle"; "Basic church doctrine"; "Prayer"; "How to exercise gifts"; "Resolution and conflict;" "How to assess student need;" "How to use creativity in the classroom and in ministries"; "How to evangelize"; "How to read and study the Bible, including history of the Bible"; "Training workers—assistants and secretarial staff"; "Recruitment for staff"; "Survey pastor"; "Survey deacons"; "Survey leaders/teachers"; "Survey student/participants"; "Survey church"; and "Self-evaluation."

# CHAPTER 5

# How to Develop a Curriculum in the American African Church

D eveloping a curriculum is still challenging for the African American church, because many churches do not have curriculum writers; some churches, moreover, will not consider encouraging nonprofessional Christian education leaders to seek training in Christian education. Questions often faced by directors will be discussed in this chapter: What is a curriculum in the church? What are some insights for developing the Christian education curriculum? Who develops or revises curriculum content? Should the curriculum include content for ministries other than the Sunday school and Bible studies? How can the DCE develop or modify already existing educational curricula for educational ministries in the African American church? How can a committee or board assist in curricula planning? What points should be considered in developing a curriculum model?

## Definitions of the Term *Curriculum*

Board or committee members may learn how to develop curriculum by attending scheduled meetings. A Christian curriculum is defined in many ways. **The DCE should understand that the term *curriculum* means the whole life and ministry of the church. The curriculum includes the participants and materials. The participants include both active and non-active parishioners. The resources for the curriculum include materials written by the congregation as well as purchased materials, classroom plans, teachers and pupils, plans for all ministry events, and textbooks.**

In *Christian Education—Foundations for the Future*, Lin Johnson states D. Campbell Wyckoff's definition of curriculum materials: "Curriculum materials consist of suggestions and resources to be used to guide, inform, and enrich the teaching-learning process as individuals and groups undertake that process" ( 496). Sunday school curricula should be our road map for the Christian life. A curriculum makes possible a lifetime of learning. In *Harper's Encyclopedia of Religious Education*, H. A. Archibald explains in his section on "Curriculum" that the word comes from the Latin word *racecourse* and alternatively "career," or the course of one's life (174). In *Fashion Me a People: Curriculum in the Church*, Maria Harris' foreword emphasizes how curriculum is the practice of fashioning a people (10). Harris says: "The curriculum is both more basic and more profound. It is the entire course of the church's life, found in the fundamental forms of that life" (63-64). The portrait of a Christian curriculum is first found in Acts 2:32 "All of us can tell you that God has raised Jesus to life." Jesus' curriculum is found in John 17:8: "I told my followers what you told me, and they accepted it. They know that I came from you, and they believe that you are the one who sent me."

Joe Marlow, reminds us of five broad definitions of curriculum. 1. Curriculum is the content made available to students (Dwayne Huebner); 2. Curriculum is the planned and guided experiences of students (John Dewey); 3. Curriculum is the actual experiences of a student or participant (Alice Miel); 4. Generally, curriculum includes both the materials and experiences for learning. Specifically, curriculum is the written courses for study used for Christian education (Iris Cully); 5. Curriculum is the organization of learning activities guided by a teacher with the intent of changing behavior (Lois Lebar).

## Insights for Developing the Christian Education Curriculum

Developing the Christian education curriculum is not easy. The African American church has needs that other churches might not envision. The average black family is now supported by a single parent. Many churches are flooded with single parents and widows. The African American church needs a curriculum that is not only holistic, but also meets special needs. The African American church must seek to recover the lost boys and girls who are on the streets. The Christian education program must provide a curriculum to revitalize the family. In *Mapping Christian Education Approaches to Congregational Learning,* Jack L. Seymour comments: "Christian education provides a context in which people engage life with the great traditions of faith, religious experiences, and the resources of our cultures" (11).

As we look at culture, African Americans should consider their own culture in America and their culture in Africa. Jack Seymour also states: "We must confront issues together by joining into the fray of history as a time full of possibility. The church must enter into the terror with the proclamation that the God of history knows the pain and suffers with us" (17). Too often, parishioners and persons in the community feel that they, too, suffer alone. Oftentimes, those in the community feel that the church is the last place that they want to attend because the curriculum does not meet the needs of parishioners and the community. In spite of one's needs, the curriculum should also provide ways to help us to understand that God knows and suffers with us (1 Peter 5:1).

In "God's Viewpoint of Christian Education," Dr. Benjamin Johnson, states, "The important components of Christian education are the teacher, the student, and the material. The Bible is also about God as our teacher" (5). He further says, "Christian education is a process of training people to act out what they have been taught from the Supreme textbook, the Bible" (5). These statements remind us that most of our time spent in ministry meetings should be spent teaching the Bible to our ministry attendees and teaching attendees how to go forth and allow Scripture to work in the lives of people. This means that the African American church can no longer depend solely on pulpit preaching to soothe the congregation's spirits and to equip people to make the Bible alive. Preaching is only one way to learn the Word, but the preached and heard Word must then be lived. The curriculum must take its course to teach the preached Word, expand on its meaning through additional educational moments, and in our ministries teach ways for attendees to leave the church with the Bible implanted in their hearts and become a reality in our world.

The African American church has a responsibility to train ministry leaders how to empower our people. The curriculum should allow attendees to understand that the God in Scripture is alive and that Jesus is no longer on the Cross, but has risen and given us the power to exercise our gifts, heal the wounded, and bring Him the lost souls. The curriculum provides ways for one to witness, study, pray, follow Christ, and care for the whole person.

*The Christian education program encompasses all education in the church.* A better way to understand the Christian education program is to understand Christian educational ministries. *Each ministry should have its own curriculum which becomes a part of the larger Christian education curriculum.* We should be careful how we allow tutorial and computer programs that are used for nonreligious instruction to dominate our curriculum. In other words, some churches are spending so much time with after-school or tutorial programs that God's mandate is forgotten. In addition, the church needs to recall that she does not replace public or private school instruction nor should the church act as chief headquarters for helping with homework. The church should be concerned about giving homework that helps students learn more about spiritual living. This is not to say that the church should not have such programs, nor to say that the church cannot impact upon the lives of those who are not excelling in other areas of life, such as general education. If there is such a program in the church, it must be made clear that it is an extension to learning, not the agenda for the Christian education program. The African American church must be about spiritual business first rather than being a baby sitting institution.

Many pastors and DCEs discuss writing their own curriculum. Curriculum writing sounds good but is not easy. Pastors and directors should first determine congregational and community needs, look at present literature and decide if there are qualified curriculum writers or if they should be sought, either paid or volunteered. It is best to supplement literature than to write literature that might not be *sound, theological* and *understood* by students.

Even when using other literature in addition to the standard literature, keep in mind what you are using. The Christian education curriculum depends much upon the literature, but other things should also be thought about when developing a curriculum.

### The Church and Christian Education Flow Chart

A **church flow chart** is needed in the African American church because often followers attempt to assume leadership responsibilities. The flow chart should consist of the following ranks: pastor (ex-officio), church officers, and church staff (usually the DCE's name follows the pastor's name), then the church administrator and minister of music.

The *Department of Christian Education flow chart* may be in place. The DCE is responsible, with pastor's approval, to modify the chart.

A Christian Education flow chart may include names of department and ministry leaders. Positions only should appear in handbooks because names will change. The following positions with names will usually appear in a separate flow chart: pastor, DCE, salaried directors (such as the director of the youth department), Department of Christian Education representatives (chair, vice-chair and secretary), department leaders and ministry leaders.

## Who Develops or Revises the Curriculum Content?

Who develops the curriculum for the African American church? The DCE provides advice but the DCE should not develop the total curriculum. **The DCE should guide the Board of Christian Education or the select committee to develop the curriculum for the Department of Christian Education.** If there is no DCE, the church should seek educators and others who have both general educational skills and Christian educational organizational and teaching skills. The final review of the curriculum should be approved and recommended to the pastor and church for adoption. Each member of the committee is a part of the team. The team should always keep in mind that the director is serving as leader. Every member of the team can be a contributor, but the main leader should be the DCE.

## Should the Curriculum Include Content for Ministries Other Than the Sunday School and Bible Study?

The curriculum should not only include content for the Sunday church school and Bible study, but also for all ministries under the umbrella of Christian education. Some churches do not see the need to think about curricula for departmental ministries such as Single Adult, Youth, Children, Family, Arts, Young Adults, and Adults.

## How Can the DCE Develop or Modify the Educational Curricula?

The DCE must first realize that things cannot change overnight. At the same time, the DCE must understand that steps toward change are needed for change to take place. It may well mean that the DCE needs to provide the pastor and church with strengths and weaknesses of the educational program. Hopefully, the pastor and church will be stimulated to make some changes. The DCE should keep in mind that the entire list may be long, because it encompasses the whole Christian education program, the Sunday church school, and all ministries under Christian education. It is then wise for the DCE to seek immediate help in modifying or developing a curriculum. I suggest that a committee comprised of Christian education leaders serve in that capacity. If there is a board already in place, members of the board should work on developing or modifying the curriculum.

## Developing a Committee or Board to Assist in Curriculum Planning

The Committee or Board of Christian Education should be composed of leaders of ministry departments, including leaders of the Sunday church school. The DCE is an ex-officio member of the board. Once the board or committee is formed, the next task is teaching board or committee members about the Christian education curriculum. Chapter six discusses organizing this board.

## SEVEN POINTS TO CONSIDER WHEN DEVELOPING A CHURCH CURRICULUM MODEL

In the *Christian Education Journal*, David W. Wright in the chapter "Choosing Appropriate Curricular Models for Christian Education" reminds us that it is difficult to select any one model for any given congregation or setting. This is very true because no two churches are alike and assessments will differ. He raised a central question for all curricula developers: "What does it mean to be educated?" (28). In addition, I suggest that the following questions be considered: After assessments, what should be included in the educational program? and How are needs of those gifted students and those who are not achieving in the program being met? David W. Wright further provides insights about models, such as a classical education which teaches curriculum content and education as transmission and the model of progressive education that teaches curriculum as process and education as development. Considering the contents for model, it is important to review Claude E. Schindler, Jr.'s model in the *Christian Education Journal* from the chapter, "Planning and Achieving Curricular Excellence." He suggests components such as: God's Word; Corporate and Departmental Philosophy; Corporate and

Departmental Goals; Scope and Sequence, integrated with the Bible; Materials and textbook selection; Selection and Development of Student Assessments, and Implementation and In-Service" ( 37-43).

## 1. Types of Curricula

**Determining the type of curricula allows the DCE to look at how students should be grouped.**

In *Handbook of Research on Curriculum* Allan Glatthon suggests four types of curricula: Mastery Curriculum, Organic Curriculum, Team-Determined Enrichment Curriculum and Student-determined Enrichment. The master curriculum is determined by the team. (This is high structure and low importance.) The organic curriculum is determined by students' needs (Requires no written guide, but systematic attention is needed. This includes high importance and low structure) (28-29). The team-determined enrichment curriculum is when knowledge is good to know but not critical, and student-determined enrichment is when low structure and low importance are placed upon the curriculum. In a student-determined enrichment curriculum, the student does much of the planning.

The African American church needs a curriculum that is a combination of mastery and organic. In other words, the curriculum should be developed by the team of leaders and at the same time based on students' needs. The African American church can no longer afford a curriculum based on her desires. Students' needs are most important.

When it comes to the types of curricula for a ministry department, needs will vary. The Sunday school may decide on the following types suggested by the authors in *Christian Education: Foundations for the Future*: **"Departmentally or group graded, closely graded, uniform, unified, and electives"** (Sloat, 498). A ministry other than the Sunday school may or may not use any of these types. For example, some ministries use a unified approach to teach all content to all ministry attendees. Each ministry should decide on the best type of curricula when considering the instructional content for the ministry.

## Clarification:

- **Departmentally or group graded** is when two or more grades or age groups study the same lesson.
- **Closely graded** is when different lessons are taught to a grade or age.

- **Uniform** is when the same Scripture passage is taught to all ages.
- **Unified** is when one Scripture theme is studied by all ages.
- **Electives** are when Scripture or topics are chosen by the class for study (Sloat, 498).

## 2. Purposes for the Curriculum

**The curriculum has various purposes, or what some call goals or aims.** Consider the purpose for your curriculum. Consider the philosophy and goals of your pastor, congregation, board, committee, the DCE and each ministry department, including the Sunday church school. **The purpose for the curriculum should tell participants what is intended.**

In *Christian Education Journal*, Claude E. Schindler, Jr. provides many suggested corporate goals for one to consider. They include: Teaching self-discipline (1 Timothy 4:7; 1 Corinthians 9:24-27); Teaching that the Holy Bible is the inspired and only infallible authoritative Word of God (2 Timothy 3:15-17 and 2 Peter 1:20-21); Lead students to confess sins (Romans 10: 9-10); Teaching students to never neglect God's will (Romans 12:1-2; 2 Timothy 2:14; and Deuteronomy 26: 16-17); Teach the importance for studying the Word of God (2 Timothy 2:15) and, Discuss the doctrines of the Bible (Titus 2:1) (39). These suggested aims are using the Bible as the primary textbook. In addition to corporate goals, individual goals are needed.

Individual goals should also be considered. These goals should include educating all persons according to needs that exist, personal strengths and weaknesses, including individual attitudes, self-motivation, available resources to assist during crisis moments, and spiritual depletion and goals for spiritual growth and living environments.

It is important for the curriculum developer to make sure that the Bible is the important part of the curriculum. In *How to Develop a Department of Christian Education in the Local Church*, Alvin C. Bernstein comments about various assumptions which guide the task (7-9). The most important belief is the Bible. The Bible is the foundation for every Christian educational curriculum.

The *United Methodist Resource Guide on Curriculum* provides more specific purposes for the curriculum. A guide published by the United Methodist Church reminds us that the curriculum should help us:

> To enlarge our grasp of the Bible, to commune with God, to appropriate and renew our tradition, to take part in the church's nurture

and mission, to receive God's grace and grow in faith, to take up our ministry, to make ethical decisions, to serve as stewards of God's gifts, to work toward common goals, and to communicate our faith. (*United Methodist Resource Guide on Curriculum*—When an Editor Looks at Content) (Printed by permission of Curricuphone)

## 3. Principles for Developing a Curriculum

**Principles provide us with the assumptions that the curriculum makes about the nature of education.** Principles determine the choices and outcomes of the existing curriculum. In *Christian Education: Foundations for the Future*, Lin Johnson provides four major principles that D. Campbell Wyckoff suggests for developing curriculum: **context, scope, purpose and process** (497).

## Clarification:

**The context** determines the setting in which the curriculum will be used. The African American church understands that her focus should primarily be African Americans; however, the setting may include non-African Americans. The African American church should consider creating a curriculum not only for African Americans but for all persons in the congregation and community. The context also refers to the group, language, culture, locale (497). **The scope** is the content needed for the various age levels. The scope should include gender considerations so that curriculum is not specifically designed for boys or girls, younger and older adults (497). **The purpose** of curriculum is to teach people the Great Commission: to make disciples and to become more like Christ (497). The curriculum should always include content to teach one how to become a disciple. **The process** of the curriculum is the way in which the content will be communicated. The methods are very important (497-98).

## 4. Characteristics of a Curriculum

**These characteristics help us review the curriculum content in what I call a wholesome way. It produces a "sound" curriculum.** D. Campbell Wyckoff helps us to understand the characteristics or standards for selecting the church curriculum. In *Christian Education —Foundations for the Future*, he speaks about seven important elements for the curriculum: **"Biblical and theological soundness,**

Relevance, Comprehensiveness, Balance, Sequence, Flexibility, and Correlation" (499).

## Clarification:

**Biblical and theological soundness** is making sure that Christianity is taught. **Relevance** is making sure the teaching reflects the needs and nature of learners in their current situation. **Comprehensiveness** means that the curriculum includes all that is essential in the scope, and that learners have developed a well-rounded Christian personality. **Balance** is teaching both Old and New Testaments. **Sequence** is the order of the curriculum content; it should be presented in a logical order for learning the content. **Flexibility** is the adaptability to meet the needs of learners, leaders and teachers. **Correlation** is when one part of the curriculum relates to the other (499).

## 5. Forms of Curriculum

**Forms of curriculum help us shape the curriculum.** Maria Harris provides discussion about three forms of curricula: **"The Explicit Curriculum, the Implicit Curriculum, and the Null Curriculum"**(68-69).

Curriculum developers should consider these three forms of the curriculum when developing or revising a curriculum.

## Clarification:

**The explicit curriculum** is what is to be presented or offered. **The implicit curriculum** means the attitudes, the procedure, the time frame and the design of the rooms. **The null curriculum** is what is absent or what is not presented. It is a paradox. This curriculum exists because something else does not exist. It could be omitted themes, omitted procedures or components needed for the overall curriculum (Harris 68-69). She explains "Where education is the fashioning and refashioning of these forms in interplay, curriculum is the subject matter and processes that make them to be what they are" (64). It then means that the content for the African American church Christian education program should be studied, carefully thought through, and reviewed with much prayer. She also provides forms of the vocation that the curriculum should end up doing: **political work of didache**

(teaching), leiturgia (prayer), koinonia (community), kerygma (proclamation), and diakonia (service).

## Forms of the Vocation That the Church Should See Embedded in the Curriculum

In *Fashion Me a People*, Maria Harris discusses how the church has already been engaged in the curriculum. She reminds the church to rephrase and reform the curriculum to meet needs of today's parishioners (68). The vocation is the work of the curriculum that should be seen in the community. **The curriculum must provide content that students can take back into the community to reach, teach and help make disciples.** Maria Harris refers to the following forms of vocation "**Curriculum of Proclamation, Curriculum of Teaching, Curriculum of Prayer, Curriculum of Community, and Curriculum of Service**" (68-69).

**The Curriculum of Proclamation** deals with the Life, Death, and Resurrection of Jesus Christ (1 Corinthians 1:23, and Acts 2-13, Luke 4:16-19). It also deals with the Bible versions, the theology, the preaching, priestly listening, and prophetic speech. The theology is what one believes, such as, about God, Jesus, and the Holy Spirit. The priestly deals with the sacramental aspect. In *Reshaping Religious Education: Conversations on Contemporary Practice*, Harris explains about the priestly and prophetic. "For even as priestly activity anoints, celebrates, heals and blesses the body, so too must educational forms be appropriate to human beings during all the bodily changes of life (27). Understanding the priestly role in the curriculum is very important because leaders should account for affirmations and the atonement. She adds:

> This means that memory must be a companion of both affirmation and atonement. As affirmation, memory celebrates and incorporates the past... As atonement, however, memory acknowledges the mistakes of the past; it acknowledges that with the good of the past has come the evil of the past. As a part of the priestly activity, both repentance and forgiveness are needed as preludes to reshaping the future. (27)

The prophecy is also very important to understand. Prophecy comes from speaking (Isaiah 6:6) (*Reshaping*, 28). The curriculum must speak in a way to help hurting people. Christian education must address ways and resources to help hurting people. Some people are buried because the Christian education program failed to suggest another means for living. All people should be considered: the incarcerated, the abused, the widows, the sick and shut-in, the homeless, the unemployed, those who live in poor conditions and those in nursing homes and mental institutions. This is no easy task. **The ultimate goal of the curriculum is to train others to serve those who are in need and at the same time to continue to educate those who are serving**.

**The Curriculum of Teaching** deals with your teaching methods. **The Curriculum of Prayer** is about Christians being in constant contact with God. **The Curriculum of Community** is helping the family and community to become closer to God. **The Community of Service** is ministering activities of the community and serving people. *Reshaping Religious Education* further elaborates on the **Curriculum of Community**. Harris adds, "That community gathers for two main purposes: to worship God through liturgical prayer and to engage in works that serve justice—the traditions of *leiturgia* and *diakonia*" (21). Interesting enough Harris speaks about the community as everyone in the congregation, certain age groups, families, including the divorced, the Lazarus groups, the need for justice group, the widowed and mourners who bury the dead, are all what she calls the community (21). The curriculum then should provide teachable materials for all persons.

Too long have many African American church curricula failed to assist mourners. The church should provide ways to reach out to all hurting people. There is no condition so tragic that God cannot solve. The curriculum should allow mourners to look at situations as a part of a learning experience and to allow the community to move a step higher to new ways of living. Lastly, when one thinks of forms, Maria Harris shares another helpful point for us, looking at the curriculum from a political view. Politically speaking, the curriculum should remind people about the power—the *Adonai*. Harris states:

> Those of us who are heirs to the biblical traditions need to keep in mind that the work of lordship is a work of governance and of creating forms that make a body into a body politic. The political dimension of a curriculum is related to our using forms that include legislation, and judicial review, and executive decisions, and reallocation of resources. (28)

## 6. Suggested Content for the African American Curriculum

**The curriculum content should include all the subjects to be taught to the church community.** The first thing to do is to think about what should be included in the curriculum content. Thoughts should be first around the aims of the church, the pastor, the DCE, department and ministry leaders. Then glance at the subjects that are often included in some curricula. These subjects may or may not be subjects to meet the DCE's needs. Decisions for selecting subjects should be made after the survey and ministry evaluation process. When considering content subjects, the seven points listed may be helpful.

### Thinking About the Curriculum Content

The African American church should consider the entire educational curriculum. This curriculum should include three aims, the first two which Gabriel Moran states in *Reshaping Religious Education: Conversations on Contemporary Practice*: "To teach people to practice a religious way of life, and to teach people to understand religion." The African American church should teach students to practice and live as Christians and at the same time, understand the religion they are affiliated with. A third aim is to motivate people to take time to sit and comprehend that learning takes place within the self and through others, introducing students to a learning environment such as the classroom. Learning includes practicing what has been taught and accepting people without concluding that your understanding of Scripture is the only way to interpret a passage.

The African American church is a change agent for creating a "newness" for ministry meetings. The "old" way of meeting to socialize, to gather community news, should no longer be the priorities for the church. Community ties have changed, family lifestyles are different, and modern ways in education have become a priority for many African American parents. The church should rethink curriculum development.

Community ties are very different as we enter the twenty-first century. Communities are interested in teaching children about safety, how to form friendships, how to select role models, and how to return unity among community members. The church curriculum should address community issues from a Christian perspective.

In *Mapping Christian Education—Approaches to Congregational Learning*, Jack Seymour states: "Christian education provides a context in which people engage life with the great traditions of faith, religious experiences, and the resources of our cultures" (11). He further elaborates : "We must confront issues together by joining in the fray of history as a time full of possibility. The church must enter into terror with the proclamation that the God of history knows the pain and suffers with us" (17). These community issues could lead the church to examine lifestyles of today. Various lifestyles are seen among church parishioners. The church has to develop a curriculum that will teach love for all people, regardless of their lifestyles and at the same time, teach Christians how to distinguish living righteously from living in sin.

The church should not endorse any lifestyle that the Bible does not endorse. In *Mapping Christian Education—Approaches to Congregational Learning*, Margaret Ann Crain comments about our responsibility to teach and our conviction. "If we do not continue to teach people what it means to be Christian, the faith will soon die out... Christian educators—whether lay, professional, ordained—begin with the conviction that God's grace goes before us" (98). The method used to teach parishioners will determine the "loss" or "gain" of the member. The curriculum should teach biblical truths in a way that persons can learn and consider upgrading their spirituality. The curriculum then should be carefully developed, thought through to meet the needs of the church and community. This concern should lead the curriculum developer to carefully plan and select educational strategies.

More and more church members are showing aspirations for developing their spiritual lives and advancing to a better lived life. Each ministry department should consider "rethinking" its purpose and the long-range goals for the ministry department. What will each ministry under the departments, such as the youth department, do to enhance one's life? Leaders should think about assessments, what works for the ministries, what turns ministry members "on" or "off," how to recover lost members, how to invite new members, and to fulfill God's will. Leaders then should consider the agenda for meetings, the content to be taught, the workshops needed and the limit upon fun activities. For example, having too many fun activities as opposed to learning activities, might not motivate members to change and live wholesome lives. In other words, bowling or going to the movies may be included as a treat or time to gather socially, but bowling or going to the movies should not be the main ingredient of the curriculum. God's Word should take precedence. When the church focuses upon her curriculum, ministry meetings will become more than "times to come together."

The curriculum can provide many ways for educating church parishioners. The curriculum should consider the development of the person. In *Mapping Christian Education—Approaches to Congregational Learning*, Maria Harris and Gabriel Moran comment on the development of the person. "For the development of the person, a Christian form of education should provide two kinds of outer activity that complement the spiritual disciplines: the study of Christian sources and the performance of Christian service. Both activities are endless in the sense of not having an endpoint; both activities deserve to be included under education" (70). The curriculum should consider not only sources but allow individuals to go into the community and make disciples. The African American church must maintain a teaching agenda to help not only those who attend church but to send those who know Christ to help bring others into the educational setting. This means that educators should consider modern educational interests. The old teaching methods might not interest students of today. It is then vital for the curriculum to include a variety of topics, methods, and means to educate today's African Americans.

## Glancing at Content Subjects

The African American church should determine its content based on ministry needs. Some of the following topics may be applicable to ministries in the African American church. Each ministry department, after deciding on its purpose, should determine the desired content. Ministry Curriculum content will differ because each ministry usually has a different focus.

The African American church may consider the following subjects when developing content for the African American church's

Christian education curriculum: The **Bible:** all subjects such as Wonder Stories, Healings and Miraculous Events, Historical Records, Holy Spirit, Heaven and Hell, Prayer, Fasting, Demons and Principalities, Spiritual Strength, and Commandments. The Bible is the main ingredient for any church curriculum. There are also other subjects that should be a part of a curriculum content in the African American church: **African history; history of the church; Baptist polity; family and community guidance; teachings about denominations; religions and cults; current life issues; printed Christian literature that will be used for the ministry; including the Sunday church school under the Board of Christian Education; needs of students; teacher concerns; supplies (including equipment to be used); materials on substance abuse; drugs and alcohol; general skills (GED, continuing education, after-school tutorials); health issues; recreation; relieving stress; employment and unemployment workshops; self-esteem workshops; how to make wise decisions for living; understanding self and community; computer classes; special concerns for boys, girls, single parents, and widows; customs; environment; social and economic standards; advanced students' needs, and special students' needs.**

### 7. An Assessment and Implementation for Service

**The assessment requires finding facts that will help in assisting students. The implementation is the action or ways for assisting students.**

It is important to provide an assessment of the community, church, ministry, leaders, and students to learn what the needs really are. Once assessments are completed and needs are known, leaders can then develop a sound curriculum. After the content has been taught, students should then be ready to provide service to others. Galatians 5:13 and Romans 12:10 are Scriptures to remind us about service to others.

### Board of Christian Education or Committee Curriculum Planning Meetings

Committee meetings may be held to organize or reorganize your Department of Christian Education. A committee may review, but not be limited to the following, at designated meetings with all members.

The DCE should provide a lot of training for these series of meetings. These meetings must be guided by the DCE. Meetings should not last longer than two hours. They should be held about once a month. It will usually take six months to one year to organize plans for developing a curriculum. Detail planning should begin shortly after the organization plan has been approved by the proper person(s). The DCE may suggest calendar dates for all meetings; however, the team should decide on dates and times. An agenda should be prepared for each meeting. Begin each meeting on time. Have different people to volunteer for the devotional period. It is important during this period to give extended time for the entire board and for mini groups to have prayer time. The first two meetings should be about three weeks apart. The third meeting should be an extended meeting with lunch or dinner served, about two months after the second meeting. The fourth meeting should be about one month after the third meeting. Three months should lapse between the fifth and six meetings.

A leader should be selected for this group. The leader for this project should not be the DCE or chair/vice-chair, but a nominated ministry leader. Again the DCE is the ex-officio to make all final approvals. In the case of an established Board of Christian Education, the chair and vice-chair should serve as regular members. This is done so that leaders will not feel like they are working under pressure of leadership. The curriculum is developed by all leaders of ministries.

## A Sample Curriculum Policy

The New Light Baptist Church has responsibility and authority for developing the Department of Christian Education ministries curriculum within the limits specified by the Department of Christian Education and approved by the church. The pastor and/or church officers and DCE will approve all instructional materials for the church.

## FIRST MEETING: CURRICULUM TERMS, DISCUSS THE MODEL (PHILOSOPHIES AND GOALS), MODEL CONTENT (THE SEVEN COMPONENTS LISTED), SHOW AN EXAMPLE OF A CURRICULUM PLAN, AND DEVELOP SURVEY QUESTIONS

This meeting is really to set the standards for all upcoming meetings. Have a devotional period and distribute an agenda for future meetings.

Dates/times/places of meetings should be decided by the group. The purpose of each meeting should be stated. The board or committee is to plan the Christian education curriculum for the church.

## Review Terms

The DCE should not assume that members of the team know the meaning of Christian educational terms. It is important for the DCE to review terms that will help the team become familiar with Christian education. Terms include: Christian education, curriculum, model, ministry, survey, goals and objectives, and any term that will describe the work of Christian education.

In addition to this, in the *Christian Education Journal*, Joe Marlow reminds us of about five important terms to discuss when planning curriculum: "curriculum, curriculum resources, curriculum design, curriculum plan and curriculum scope" (70). After this discussion, the committee or board should be asked to attend the upcoming meeting with their ministry goals.

It is helpful to work in small groups. Leaders from each ministry should return to their ministry department and work with their leaders, teaching them how to develop goals and plan for their ministry. Members should also be assigned to meet with their department and develop survey questions, which will be given to the department for both workers and students at the next ministry meeting.

## The Model

The model is a key point to discuss. The model includes the philosophies and goals of the community, church, pastor, the director of Chrisitan education, Department of Christian Education, and ministry departments, including the Sunday church school. Usually when one studies the philosophies and goals, glance at another curriculum for suggestions and start thinking and developing survey questions, then one is well on the way to planning curriculum. This is a good time for the DCE to provide definitions and examples of goals and philosophies. The DCE should also remind all members of this team how important it is to remember the age groups and learning levels. Review the "Seven Points to Consider When Developing a Church Curriculum Model."

## The Model Content

The DCE should now discuss some suggested content for each ministry curriculum. It is best to meet with each ministry leader to share content that may be found for that ministry. The DCE will inform leaders that the content is developed only after surveys have been completed and the ministry has been evaluated. For example, youth ministry should include content for youth, adult ministry should include content for adults. Ministry leaders should keep in mind the ages, grade levels and learning levels in which the curriculum will be used, the ethnicity, culture, and environment. Review Point 6 under "Seven Points to Consider When Developing a Church Curriculum Model."

## Examples of a Curriculum Plan

The DCE should show examples of a working curriculum structural plan. If one cannot find a church curriculum, one might speak to a high school and elementary principal to borrow or copy a public school curriculum. Speak to both principals to review curricula for the various ages, through age eighteen. Spend several hours to reshape the vision of the pastor, church, DCE, and Board or Committee of Christian Education. Review the strengths and weaknesses of the past twenty-five years of the present curriculum, and strengths and weaknesses of the goals presented. Decide where the church is and her strengths and weaknesses since Christian education has been a part of the church, even if the church only started with a Sunday school. Decide where the church really is and where she is headed the next five and ten years.

## Survey Questions

The DCE should allow members of the committee to work in groups to develop survey questions for the following areas: ministry leaders, ministry students or attendees of the ministry, members of the church, ministers of the church, church leaders (deacons, deaconesses, trustees). The DCE should suggest some questions about each area. Then, allow the subcommittee to work on this project (on their own time) and present typed questions to the DCE before the next meeting.

# SECOND MEETING: REVIEW THE MODEL (PHILOSO-PHIES, GOALS), AND SURVEY QUESTIONS, AND DECIDE ON WAYS TO DEVELOP, DISTRIBUTE AND COLLECT SURVEY QUESTIONS

## Review the Model (Philosophies and Goals)

Once you have decided on the model that best serves your church, review all philosophies and goals for the curricula.

## Discuss Developing the Survey Questions

This meeting will allow ministry leaders to discuss developing survey questions. The DCE should have some knowledge of how to develop questionnaires. Survey questions should be developed for each area (see point five). It is wise to show a sample survey. The committee or board should make suggestions for improvement. The final survey questions should be typed and distribution procedures discussed. Final copies should be distributed to the entire team. The DCE should make final suggestions and recommendation to the pastor and church.

## Discuss Ways to Distribute, Collect, Talley Survey Questions and Writing of the Final Survey Report

The DCE should review how to distribute and collect survey questions, tally the results, and write the final report. It is best to distribute questions to ministry leaders and ministry attendees at the same time. Attendees will not feel threatened when they and leaders are completing a form for education. It is very important to explain the urgency of this matter. Ministers and leaders of the church may be given survey questions at their upcoming meeting. Have the leader of each team to be responsible for distributing and collecting the surveys by a certain deadline. The pastor will suggest the best time to distribute survey questions to the congregation. The important key is to be given a time to collect them immediately after they have been completed.

No name needs to be given by those completing survey questions.

The final analysis should be given to the DCE and to each member of the committee. The DCE should review and provide the pastor with a copy.

## THIRD MEETING: REVIEW SOME POINTS FOR CURRICULUM DEVELOPMENT, REVIEW NAMES OF ALL MINISTRIES OF THE CHURCH AND BEGIN PLANNING FOR EACH CHRISTIAN EDUCATIONAL MINISTRY

### Review Points for Developing the Curriculum

### Review Names of the Church's Present Ministries

The DCE should review some ministries that come under Christian education. Some ministries may need to be placed under a different heading or moved into a different department. Usually, if the director does not seem "pushy," the team will concur with the leader. Remember, final placement must be approved by the pastor. This includes adding or moving a ministry department.

### Suggested Ministries Under the Board of Christian Education

Ministries will vary from church to church. If a church does not have active ministries and wants to form new ministries within the church, it is better to start with a few ministries before creating more ministries than the DCE and church can supervise. The following are some **suggested ministries under the Board of Christian Education: Cultural Enrichment (theater, dance and African history); Health Ministry (aids ministry, enlightenment classes and fitness classes); Young Adult Ministry; Adult Ministry; Singles Ministry; Children's Ministry; Youth Ministry; Basic Membership (new membership classes, extended membership classes and Big Brothers and Big Sisters ministry); Bible Study Ministry (Bible studies for all age groups and various topics/classes per session); Leadership Development Ministry; Family Life Ministries (employment, marriage, divorce, parenting, marriage enrichment, Mother's and Father's Days, family month, single adult month, seniors month, and crisis aid); Mentoring Ministry (boys and girls learning how to select role models and to adopt role models); the Sunday Church School (the nursery, and all age level departments); and Missionary Education (how to pray, how to give to missions, how to spread the Gospel).**

The minister of music may attend board meetings because the Department of Christian Education is also responsible for co-directing educational workshops in music to educate the congregation about music, such as, how a certain hymn came into existence and the meaning of it, or a discussion about the songwriter's purpose, or discussing the various forms of music. This responsibility does not infringe upon the duty of the minister of music. The minister of music should work to co-develop such teaching with the DCE. All teaching seminars should be reviewed by the DCE.

In addition, the chair of the Missionary Board may attend board meetings because teaching workshops that teach mission and ways to evangelize should be co-developed with the DCE. The missionary is responsible for sending, but instruction comes from the Board of Christian Education. Again, the DCE must maintain his or her own work, without interference from other departments.

### Some Possible Headings Under Pastoral Work

The work of the pastor can be understood only by the pastor and congregation. Such duties will vary from church to church. The pastor may be in charge of membership development; directing or teaching black presence in the Bible; the undershepherd (Jesus is the Head Shepherd) of the entire church/congregational needs; seeing that teachings are on denominational views, the church's history, and church doctrine; counseling; setting the agenda for deacons, deaconesses, the ministerial staff, and all other employees; directing, in many cases, Children and Youth Churches. The Christian education department should teach evangelism, but should also understand that the Missionary Department provides the "sending" for missionary work.

### Some Possible Headings Under Mission Ministry

The mission ministry involves evangelism (the teaching and the sending). Groups or individuals may be sent on foreign missions. The purpose of mission education is to educate leaders who have knowledge of Christian education to "go forth." The Christian education team equips leaders with content, the mission ministry trains leaders how to use the content.

Then the DCE should go over points about developing a church curriculum and discuss content for various ministries. It will be helpful to provide a bibliography, tapes or other materials that will not conflict with your denominational views. When in doubt, ask the pastor for advice. Each leader can now be assigned the responsibility to return to his or her ministry and begin researching, reading and planning for the ministry. It is wise for the DCE to set up meetings with individual department/ministry leaders to suggest ideas and listen to presented ideas. Typed draft reports should be submitted to the DCE. The DCE may make suggestions and request two to three drafts before approving the report. The final report will then be submitted at the upcoming meeting for team review and discussion.

### Planning for Each Ministry

These results will determine the needs for the ministries in Christian education. From the results, a committee can decide on components needed for developing a curriculum in the church. Even though each leader will decide on components for his or her curriculum, the committee can share ideas with leaders. The DCE should require each department leader to submit a content proposal for its ministry group. Upon the DCE's review and pastor's approval, the department leader can meet with its ministry leaders to begin developing its curriculum.

## FOURTH MEETING: EACH MINISTRY PRESENTS A DRAFT OF CURRICULUM IDEAS FOR REVIEW

In this meeting, all members of the team will look at the work of all ministries. Many times, when one is not involved in a certain ministry, one can suggest things that those involved cannot see. This meeting may take some time, but it will be well worthwhile. The DCE should also teach each team member how to write the final plan.

## FIFTH MEETING: WRITING THE CURRICULUM PLAN

At this point, allow each department leader about three months to meet with his or her ministry leaders to rewrite their ministry curriculum plan. When writing curriculum, one may seek help from a trained curriculum specialist. Include plans for the next three years for your ministry. For each year, each ministry should state its ministry philosophy and goals for the ministry; objectives for each ministry (goal and objectives of the department and from the specific needs of students in the ministry); how the goal and objectives will be met; workshop topics; forums; symposiums for the ministry; calendar for the ministry—all meeting dates for the next three years, all activities that will be used (at least an overview if activities are not named); types of field trips; retreats; and camps; book titles and if available; samples of literature (if no samples, book titles and descriptions, including the names of publishers and the type of literature to be used).

Each department leader should return to its ministry to develop the final curriculum plan. Submit the typed plan to the DCE. The DCE should suggest meeting dates for each leader and establish a deadline for the curriculum plan.

## SIXTH MEETING: FEEDBACK FROM THE CURRICULUM PLAN

After the committee has critiqued each other's work (Department Leaders), the committee may then move to provide closure for the meetings. Each department leader should submit a final draft of its curriculum to the DCE. The DCE will review and make comments for improvement. A final copy should be given to the DCE. The pastor and/or deacons may review and recommend changes. Each ministry curriculum becomes a part of the whole. All curricula plans become as one curriculum for the department.

## SEVENTH MEETING: TESTING THE CURRICULUM

Each department leader will test a component of the curriculum with its ministry. This is to make sure that it will meet the needs of the ministry. If it seems to work, write up the draft of the curriculum. If the component taught does not seem to work, work on a new idea and continue to test other ideas. It may mean that many components should be tested when one component is not working. In other words, if the components or ideas do not meet the needs of the learners, it is not working.

## Using the Curriculum

Once the curriculum has been decided upon, consider ways of using the curriculum. The misuse of any curriculum is just as bad as not having any curriculum to follow. Most needed is prayer, meditation, and sensing how God wants pieces of the curriculum taught at certain meetings. The Religious Education Curriculum Project described in the book, *Religious Education Teaching Approaches,* provides three considerations when using the curriculum: lesson planning, language and communication, and the range of content.

The developers of curriculum are responsible for their lessons. The teaching method can make good curriculum content better understood or misunderstood. Ministry leaders need to carefully plan their ministry instructional time. At the same time, the language and communication matter.

The language, which reflects the way one teaches, will often determine if a student can understand the points discussed. Ministry leaders should give much thought to their language and communication. Will ministry members understand the teaching, or will they leave the ministry meeting confused? Knowing how to use right language and communication skills will allow the ministry leader and teacher to choose the appropriate content.

The range of content in the church should serve two purposes: primary and secondary. The primary range is to teach the Bible. The next purpose is to teach people how to exercise what has been taught.

# SOURCES CITED

Archibald, H. A. " Curriculum" in *Harper's Encyclopedia*. Cully, Iris V. and Kendig Brubaker, editors. second edition. San Francisco: Harper and Row, 1971.

Bernstein, Alvin. *How to Develop a Department of Christian Education Within the Local Church*. Nashville: Townsend Press, 1995.

Glatthorn, Allan. *Handbook of Research on Curriculum*. New York: Maxmillian, 1992.

_____*Developing a Quality Curriculum*. Alexandria, Virginia: Association for Supervision and Curriculum Development, 1994.

Harris, Maria and Moran, Grabriel. *Reshaping Religious Education: Conversations on Contemporary Practice*. Louisville: Westminister John Knox Press, 1998.

Johnson, Benjamin. "God's Viewpoint of Christian Education" in *Christian Education Informer*: Sunday School Publishing Board. 50:1 (June-August 1997): 5.

Johnson, Benjamin. "God's View Point of Christian Education." *A Manual for Leadership Education and Curriculum Guide*. Nashville: Sunday School Publishing Board, 1994.

Johnson, Lin. "Understanding and Using Curriculum." *In Christian Education: Foundations for the Future*, Robert E. Clark, et al, editors. Chicago: Moody Press, 1991.

Marlow, Joe. D. "Choosing Appropriate Curricular Models for Christian Education" in *Christian Education Journal*. 15:2. Winter, 1995.

——————— "Analyzing the Curriculum Debate." 13:3. (Spring, 1993): 95. *Religious Education Teaching Approaches*. Australia: Queensland: Curriculum Services Branch, Department of Education, 1987.

Seymour, Jack L. "Approaches to Christian Education" in *Mapping Christian Education—Approaches to Congregational Learning*. Nashville: Abingdon Press, 1997.

Schindler, Claude E., Jr. "Planning and Achieving Curricular Excellence" in *Christian Education Journal*. Scripture Press Ministries. 9:1. Autumn, 1988.

Pamphlet "When an Editor Looks at Content." Nashville: Graded Press—United Methodist Publishing Board, revised 1988.

Wright, David W. "Choosing Appropriate Curricular Models for Christian Education" in *Christian Education Journal*. 15:2. Winter, 1995.

# CHAPTER 6

# Organizing a Board of Christian Education and Training Ministry Leaders

A board has the purpose to oversee the entire Christian education program in the church. Some churches have a committee that serves the same function as a board. A committee usually is a group of persons serving a short term. Board members usually serve for three or five years. The purpose of the board is to make sure that the church knows what is going on. The board reports to the DCE and deacons of the church. Some churches elect the board to report only to the DCE and church council meetings, at which deacons are represented. The board is to make sure that church doctrine is carried out and that Christian conduct is maintained. The board or committee should also see that programs are operated according to the chosen denomination by-laws and that the curriculum meets the needs of the congregation. The DCE may elect a Chair or Dean to chair meetings. The board assists the DCE with planning. The DCE usually prepares the agenda for the board. In *The Teaching Church at Work—A Manual for the Board of Christian Education*, Kenneth D. Blazier and Linda R. Isham suggest that the situation should be considered. "Each congregation will need to select the model for structuring the administration of Christian education that potentially will be most effective in its situation" (28). These authors suggest models such as a board with responsibilities, a board with responsibilities and subcommittees, a board with task groups (assigned projects), a board with flexible structure, and a church with a single board (deacons, trustees and Christian education). A board with responsibilities is recommended because leaders who represent ministries can provide suggestions, and as a team, all leaders can assist one another. Really, the church decides whether or not a board or committee is needed.

## Department Leaders and Ministry Leaders

A board consists of department leaders of ministries, including the superintendent of the Sunday church school. The **department leader** is a facilitator, an organizer, one who suggests and one who leads ministry leaders. The department leader may or may not lead activities and events. In most cases, the department leader wants to attend as many ministry meetings as possible to stay in tune with what's going on in the ministry. The department leader is responsible for student activities and events. The Director of Missions, the Music Director, Vacation Bible School leaders (VBS) are not often board members, but the education programs are reviewed by the DCE. Some writers suggest that the committee include at least two to three members from the congregation. Board members (Ministry Department Leaders) and the Sunday church school superintendent usually serve for three years. According to *A Manual for Leadership Education and Curriculum Guide* produced by the Christian Education Department of the Sunday School Publishing Board, NBC, Inc., "The board of Christian education should be composed of representatives of every phase of church life" (2).

## The Chair of Board of Christian Education

Even though a Board for Christian Education exists, it is very crucial for the DCE to comprehend the duties and purpose for the Chair of the Board of Christian Education. The Chair may be a member of the congregation. If so, the DCE supervises the Chair. In many cases, the DCE may select a Dean to guide board meetings. The Dean serves similar duties as the "Chair." If the DCE, the ex-officio, allows the Dean to lead meetings, the DCE should approve any agenda. The secretary should take written minutes (no taping because of privacy) and submit a copy within one week following the meeting to the DCE and the Chair (Dean). Board meetings may be monthly, bimonthly or quarterly, depending on the size of the church.

## Evaluating Members of the Board of Christian Education

Members of the board should be evaluated by the DCE at least once a year. In some cases, the director may allow the chair or vice chair to assist in the evaluation. Teachers and Departmental

Superintendents of the Sunday church school should be evaluated by the Superintendent. The DCE may or may not conduct his or her own evaluation of teachers and Department Superintendents.

## Responsibilities of the Board of Christian Education

The Board of Christian Education should make sure that ministries function according to the guidelines and beliefs of the church, and that ministry leaders and ministry performance are monitored. The board is also responsible for making recommendations to the DCE for filling board vacancies, monitoring performance of board members, receiving ministry reports from board members, compiling board news such as for church announcements or church bulletins and making sure that ministry leaders operate according to church guidelines. The DCE approves or may suggest the training. The board also compiles board news for church announcements and church bulletins.

## Make Recommendations to the DCE for Filling All Vacancies

Filling vacancies should never be taken lightly. It is not always easy to secure a leader who is committed to Christian education. In addition to prayer, allow God to move through board members for recommending leaders for vacant positions. Usually, a board member who cares about ministry will recommend others who also care about ministry. The DCE has the final recommendation for filling vacancies. The pastor or the DCE will give the final approval.

The recommendations should be given to the DCE, who in turn, recommends names to the pastor. Recommendations should go beyond "friends" of leaders. Many new members have experience, and upon seeing their faithfulness, should be considered as possible candidates. In most cases, a new member (one who joins by Christian experience) can usually adjust to the church setting in about one year. Requiring new members to be a member for more than a year before working in the church may be a turn off factor to new members who are ready to work. This could result in losing the member or could blur one's interest in Christian education. New converts may adjust in less than one year, but only in rare cases. New converts need to explore Sunday school classes, Bible study, and other activities as a lay person before becoming a leader. If a new convert is chosen as a leader, one should be on a team with a veteran ministry leader. In most cases, a member who has faithfully worked elsewhere will resume faithful service, especially when introduced to new possibilities.

## Compile Board News for Church Announcements

The board is responsible for education announcements that go in the church bulletin or for pulpit announcements. The board may elect such a person to collect church news from ministry leaders. The elected person is responsible for final editing; however, each ministry leader is also responsible for his or her own submitted typed news. Each department leader submits news to the person in charge of collecting news. Deadlines must be clearly explained. Many times the DCE will want to review all announcements before the publishing stage. This means that ministry news should be reported at least two to three weeks prior to the deadline for printing. However, announcements may also be placed on appropriate bulletin boards. Often naming one person to be in charge of bulletin boards makes things go smoothly. The elected person should have skills in designing nice bulletin boards. One major board may be used for announcements, since announcements may be freely posted by any member of the board or DCE. The DCE may discard any inappropriate announcements without notice. It is best to have bulletin announcements approved prior to posting them.

## Make Sure Ministries Function According to Guidelines of the Church

The board has a responsibility to make sure that ministries adhere to church guidelines. Ministries are an extension of the church. All activities must be Christian in nature and attempt to motivate one to be a better Christian. The church's constitution or by-laws is most helpful for ministries to follow. It is also very important for ministries to abide by the beliefs of the church denomination. Even though a leader might have personal views, the ministry should always uphold the beliefs of the church and denomination.

## Monitor Performance of Board Leaders and Receive Ministry Reports

Ministry leaders paid or unpaid provide a service for the Lord. All leaders need assessments. They let us know our strong and weak points in ministry. A good leader is open to constructive criticism. Ministry leaders should be evaluated at least annually. Poor performance should suggest training and giving one an opportunity to continue the assignment. If one does not make an effort to improve within a year, a recommendation should be made for the person to seek a new ministry. This recommendation has nothing to do with tenure. Ministries should also be evaluated. Ministries exist for the purpose of helping holistic spiritual growth. A growing ministry is one that seeks new ideas, new ways of operating, and ways to reach the "unreached."

## Implement Training for Board Members

Training is the key for any Board of Christian Education. Leaders need training. The Board of Christian Education is responsible for implementing training for board members. In other words, the board should see that the training is implemented, and that the needed supplies, helps, and materials are provided for the training. Teachers and assistants may be trained to carry out the training. The DCE should develop the actual training materials for board members. Two types of training are recommended: Training new leaders and in-service training for present leaders.

New leaders need to undergo an orientation that will introduce the ministry, planning, operation, and how to survive as a leader. It is best to train new leaders before the first of the calendar year or the new year, or before installation of church officers, whichever is applicable, so that new leaders will be energetic to begin with fresh ideas. After board members are trained, they can then move to the planning stage.

## Planning

Department leaders and ministry leaders should begin planning early for the upcoming year. Department leaders should provide ministry leaders with planning suggestions and be a part of the planning process. The following may be a suggested calendar for new department leaders.

**Six months** before the calendar year of service, meet with the DCE to learn about the ministry. **Four months** before your year of service, contact the present department leader to learn about the ministry. Request a copy of the calendar for the present and upcoming years, a copy of the budget for both years, a copy of the roster of students: names, addresses, phone and fax numbers of ministry leaders and workers. **Three months** before your year of service, ask to visit the ministry to observe the students. Suggest to the DCE a survey proposal for students, church leaders, ministry leaders and for parishioners. **Two months** before your time of service, contact the ministry leaders and ministry workers to meet early as possible to begin planning for the new year. **Consider at least three meetings** with ministry Leaders before your new calendar year. It is wise to stay in touch with the DCE to report how the ministry is progressing.

Both the department leader and ministry leaders should share responsibilities for ministry meetings such as the department leader may prefer working with Bible study, a ministry leader may prefer working with activities, one may prefer planning trips, while another may prefer to plan workshops or special youth days. Another leader may prefer directing youth discussions. No matter who directs one thing or the other, all leaders should equally share in the planning. There are times when more than one leader, or even all leaders, prefer to work on the same project. The planning should allow students to enjoy attending ministry meetings.

Ministry meetings should be exciting and fun for students. Students should be a part of planning ministry meetings. Leaders may meet for the ground work, but students should also share ideas. A suggested ministry for the beginning of a new year might seem difficult, but planning for the first meeting is usually challenging in planning for the year.

**WORKS CITED**

Blazier, D. Kenneth, & Isham, R. Linda. *The Teaching Church at Work—A Manual for the Board of Christian Education*. Valley Forge: Judson Press, 1993.

The Christian Education Department. *A Manual for Leadership Education and Curriculum Guide*. Nashville: Sunday School Publishing Board NBC, USA, Inc., 1994

# CHAPTER 7

# *Discussions of the English, American, and African American Sunday Schools*

T his chapter will focus on the role that the English, American and the African American Sunday schools provide in understanding the origins of the African American Sunday school. Contributions of an African American Sunday school pioneer, Katie Ferguson, will be cited.

This chapter will further allow the director to understand the Sunday school movements and to provide firsthand information in teaching congregations about the movements. A careful review of the Sunday school movement will help parishioners and those who teach them to be reminded of the importance of attending Sunday church school.

This work does not replace any historical works, nor does it attempt to be the only work on this subject, but I hope it will be a foundation for many writers to build upon. The term, *African American Sunday school,* refers to the African American church school.

## The English Sunday School

Robert Raikes organized the Sunday school in England in 1780-81, according to the *Sunday School Informer*. Raikes was a printer in Gloucester, England. By chance, he had made a trip to the outskirts of town on business. During this trip to the suburbs, he saw a large number of ragged and filthy children in the street (1-5).

In *Black Baptist Sunday School Growth*, Sid Smith reminds us that there were many harsh conditions in European cities during the Industrial Revolution. Poor and uneducated children were abused by the educated. In other words, there were no provisions for educating the poor. At the end of a work week, poor people would relax on Sundays. Many times children would wander the streets, damaging property or just being mischievous (127-28). Raikes provided children a time to learn reading, writing and other skills, all to keep them off the street.

Sid Smith further speaks about Raikes' school: "The first Sunday school proved to be an effective means of behavior modification" (126). In *The Big Little School: Two Hundred Years of the Sunday School,* Robert Lynn and Elliott Wright speak about Raikes' starting a Sunday school in England. "He started his first Sunday charity school in 1780 or 1781 by hiring a teacher to set up shop in Gloucester's Sooty Alley" (5). In *Building a Strong Sunday School,* Marcel Kellar states that a Baptist deacon, Mr. William Fox of London, England, felt that Mr. Raikes' goal was secular rather than religious, but churches placed the Bible into Sunday school transforming it into a religious and moral institution (7).

Robert Raikes discussed his purpose for establishing the Sunday school as both religious and secular. Marcel Kellar provides statements that Mr. Raikes made.

> I was expressing my concern to one at the forlorn and neglected state of the children, and was told if I were to pass through the streets on Sunday it would shock me indeed to see the crowds of children who were spending this sacred day in noise and riot to the extreme annoyance of all decent people. I was determined to make some little effort to remedy this evil. Having four persons who had been accustomed to instruct children, I engaged to pay the same sum they required for receiving and instructing such children as I should send to them every Sunday morning. The children were to go soon after ten o'clock in the morning and stay until twelve; they were then to go home and return at one and after reading the lesson they were to be instructed by the church. After church they were to be employed in reading the catechisms until half past five, and then be dismissed with the injunction to go home without making a noise, and by no means to play in the streets (6).

## The American Sunday School

The American Sunday school has been teaching Christian education for many years. There is much to be learned from the American Sunday school. It has provided many suggestions for Sunday school operation. It has provided African Americans an opportunity to glance at the various schools and to learn much about the development of the

Sunday school. The white Protestant church in America organized its Sunday school around Robert Raikes' ideas. The beginning of schools in America should be studied to learn the full "richness" of the American Sunday school. Tim Stafford states in his article, "This Little Light of Mine," that

> The first American Sunday schools were started in the 1790s, modeled on British experiments. They aimed at offering the illiterate, urban poor a basic education—reading, and writing with the Bible as textbook. Sponsored by philanthropic laypersons, these first Sunday schools usually had no institutional tie to the established church....
> They were, after all, fulfilling a secular purpose—education (30).

Stafford does not comment on the African American Sunday school as being part of the American Sunday school. In *From Sunday School to Church School: Continuities in Protestant Church Education in the United States, 1860-1929*, Jack Seymour states that in 1859, at the Third National Sunday School Convention held in Philadelphia, the Sunday school was officially recognized as a department of the church (25). He remarks that, at first, the Sunday school was referred to as a mission school (30), but that, "Since the 1820s, the Sunday school had slowly become the church's school" (31). In the beginning of the American Sunday school, some churches included their Sunday schools as a part of their institution. Meanwhile, however, African Americans were already operating their Sunday schools on a private basis.

In *The Big Little School: Two Hundred Years of the Sunday School*, Robert Lynn and Elliott Wright remind us that the American Sunday school sees Mr. Raikes as the Father of the Sunday school. "The work of Robert Raikes, known as the 'Father' of the Sunday school, began in the 1780s and quickly spread through the English speaking world" (4). **Some consider him the Father of the American Sunday school, but Mr. Raikes is not the Father of the African American Sunday school because African Americans had already received knowledge and began operating their Sunday school prior to Raikes' suggestions.**

## The African American Sunday School

It is good to report that Sunday school leaders are caring and becoming more concerned about the African American Sunday school.

Far too long has the African American church neglected the importance of the Sunday school. The African American church has been deprived of the truth about the African American Sunday school. Some African Americans have believed that the Sunday school was founded by Robert Raikes, but the origins of the African American Sunday school differ from the white Protestant church in America.

This section will highlight areas that help us glance at some origins of the African American Sunday school. In addition, we will discuss various agents of the African American Sunday school such as those groups and individuals who helped provide us a record of those origins. Some of these resources are: The Freedmen's Bureau, the role of historic churches, the Society for the Propagation for the Gospel, surveys on religious education for the African American church, the role of some denominations and conventions, and we will cite a great pioneer, Katie Ferguson. *The African American Sunday school originated from African educational roots deeply entrenched in Kemetics lifestyles.*

There are thousands of African American church organizations in the country, but when did the institution of the African American Sunday school begin? When some origins are cited, the curriculum and other insights about the Sunday school may be better understood.

## Some Origins of the African American Sunday School

In *Black Children: Their Roots, Culture, and Learning Styles*, Janice E. Hale-Benson reminds us: "Research suggests that Black people are sufficiently isolated in American society to preserve and transmit cultural patterns" (6). These cultural patterns were taught in Africa. The knowledge that African Americans have acquired has led to various forms of education.

Many of these non-Sunday school related institutions teach spiritual values and instruct us how to live and provide more and more insights for transmitting education into our Sunday schools. The Sunday school needs committed leaders such as a pastor, the director of Christian education, superintendents, teachers, and workers in the Sunday school. It takes all of these leaders and students to have a vital Sunday school.

We have very little information about dates for African American religious education because some white settlers were not concerned about such education and thus did not record it. In *Renewing the Sunday School and the CCD*, D. Campbell Wyckoff states: "Some Whites believed Blacks were too stubborn to become real Christians. Owners could not spare them to take classes, and many argued that they were too wicked anyway" (Wyckoff, 72). In spite of what was not told to our forefathers, we must do our best to examine the date and the forerunner for the African American Sunday school.

Non-African American teaching does not always meet all needs of African Americans; however, non-African Americans can teach African Americans and African Americans can teach non-African Americans. African Americans should, however, be taught from the African American perspective originating in the African American culture. Non-African American teaching must be modified to meet the needs of African Americans. The African American Sunday school must review Christian education resources to see if the publisher or group's intended use fits their purposes.

The Sunday school has always been a bridge to connect different points in one's life. On Sunday mornings, the child shares his or her daily experiences with the teacher. In his thesis, "The Study of the Sunday School: Provided for the Immediate Department of the Colored Methodist Episcopal Church," Lorenzo Brown discusses one beginning for the American Sunday school. He states, "About 1840, however, the Sunday school as an institution had gained sufficient recognition to convince religious leaders of its permanence and value" (1-4).

The teacher has an important task, as he or she has to relate the child's experiences to religion. Therefore, the teacher plays a very major role in shaping a child's spiritual life. The teacher then becomes both a Sunday school teacher and a public school teacher. In *Lift Every Voice: African American Oratory, 1787-1900*, Austin Steward, in the chapter "Termination of Slavery," remarks: "Look then to the noblest of all remedies for this evil, the Sunday school—that most useful of all institutions. There you may learn without loss of time or money, that of which none should be ignorant to read" (108).

African Americans organized their own schools, many in homes, when whites closed doors to theirs. In *Working with Carter G.*

*Woodson: the Father of Black History—A Diary 1928-1930*, Lorenzo Green states, " Puritan leaders considered it a violation of the rights of the home to have the children in Sunday school upon the Sabbath and also a most ungodly infringement upon the Lord's Day" (43). To African Americans, it meant that children had a right to attend church and Sunday school.

Anne Boylan explains in *Sunday School—The Formation of An American Institution, 1790-1880* how Frederick Douglass helped teach a Sunday school in Baltimore at the home of James Mitchell, a free colored man. Whites eventually intervened, interrupting the Sunday school and claiming that Douglass wanted to be another Nat Turner. Douglas then decided to start his own school, where he taught twenty or thirty young men to read the Bible (29). African Americans did not allow others to hinder their progress.

During slavery, African Americans were determined to continue their education. Boylan also states:

> Missionaries of the (Congregational) American Missionary Association, the Methodist Freedmen's Aid Society, the American Sunday School Union, and various home missions societies started both day and Sunday schools wherever they could, reporting back to their superiors on the extraordinary eagerness of Blacks—adults as well as children—to learn to read the Bible. African Americans were so eager to continue the Sunday school as a people.... Blacks themselves, however, asserted their desire to run their own schools and by 1870 most Southern Black Sunday schools were probably in Black hands. (29)

It takes the work of the entire church to make the Sunday school what it should be. The African American Sunday school has always been a teaching institution. The African American Sunday school is well on her way to a promising future. In *A Growing Sunday School*, Kenneth D. Blazier states: "Church school growth will take place only in churches that plan for it. Such growth is dependent upon careful planning and diligent implementation of plans" (18). More and more schools are advancing by having classes for all age levels and on various topics. I observed and interviewed various Sunday school leaders about the work of the Sunday school. Most leaders are anxious to learn more about the African American Sunday school. In *A Manual for Sunday Schools*, Charles Dinkins makes a strong point that is often forgotten. He states: "It must be kept in mind that the Sunday school is only one phase of the total educational program of the church" (7). For years, many churches did not view other ministries under the board or committee of education. It is then important for the Sunday church school to work with other ministries to plan to meet needs for the total church. For example, the Sunday school should work with the youth ministry and coordinate events as a team, because they both serve the same youth in many cases. If they do not serve the same youth, both ministries will have an opportunity to encourage all students to become a part of both ministries.

In *10 Super Sunday Schools in the Black Community*, Sid Smith discusses Dr. Willie Gaines, pastor of Emmanuel Baptist Church, San Jose, California, of the 10 Super Sunday schools. This pastor speaks about their Sunday school having six tasks: "To reach people for Bible study, to teach the Bible, to witness to persons about Christ and lead them in church membership, to lead members to worship, to minister to Sunday school members and nonmembers, and to interpret and undergird the work of the church and the denomination"(39).

The Sunday school has a major responsibility to care for souls. The African American church must consider her goals and objectives for the Sunday school. After establishing the goals and objectives, the calendar for the Sunday school should be given thought. The Sunday school should have a calendar that will meet the needs of the Sunday church school.

## Agents of the African American Sunday School

There are other persons and organizations who must be credited for the African American Sunday School Movement. In *Christian Education Journey of Black Americans: Past, Present, Future*, the late Grant Shockley discusses agents of the African American Sunday school. As early as 1678, women of the Maryland Society protested the lack of education for the African American church members. He adds, "In 1679 and again in1690, George Fox wrote to America, "And, also, you must teach and instruct blacks and Indians" (6). Grant Shockley explains that the purpose of religious education was to evangelize. About 1735, the Moravians went in many directions as evangelists. Their congregation consisted of Indians, blacks, and white settlers. In 1738, the Moravians made some attempts to organize missions for African Americans. Religious education was their main activity (7). In addition to such agents as George Fox and the Moravians, other groups and individuals help us review origins of the African American Sunday school.

## The Role of the Freedmen's Bureau in the Origins of the African American Sunday School

In *The Black Church and the Black Experience*, John Blackwell speaks well of the Freedmen's Bureau. The Freedmen's Bureau established more than 500 schools and colleges for African Americans all over the South (47-48). The Freedmen's Bureau deserves credit for encouraging many to organize Sunday schools.

Donald G. Nieman, in *To Set the Law in Motion: The Freedmen's Bureau and the Legal Rights of Blacks 1865-1868*, applauds the Bureau for its efforts to help blacks. In March 1865, the Freedmen's Bureau Act was passed as a temporary agency for the War Department "to continue during the present war of rebellion, and for one year thereafter "(4). This bureau provided blacks with legal protection when the Antebellum Southern state law had discriminated against blacks. As a result, African Americans were able to do many things that they had been denied, including practicing their right to worship and to become educated. In *Negro Americans in the Civil War: From Slavery to Citizenship*, Charles Wesley and Patricia Romero comment on the Freedmen's Bureau.

> Education was not a stated function of the Freedmen's Bureau when it was first established; but by the amended act of July 16, 1866, this became one of its authorized purposes... Schools were soon started for Negroes and whites, under the auspices of the bureau, comprising day, night, Sabbath and summer schools. (132)

The Bureau was helpful in educating African Americans in more than one way, including to set higher standards for the Sunday school. In *From Slavery to Freedom: A History of African Americans*, editors of the chapter state: ["The Effort to Attain Peace," also states the Freedmen's Bureau's purpose:] "The bureau achieved its greatest successes in education. It set up or supervised all kinds of schools: day, night, Sunday, and industrial schools as well as colleges" (230).

## The Society for the Propagation of the Gospel: Other Early Influences on the African American Sunday Church School

The African American Sunday school has an outstanding opportunity to teach because of the influence from numerous groups and societies. One of these societies is the Society for the Propagation of the Gospel.

Dr. Colleen Birchette remarks in her article, "A History of Religious Education in the Black Church," that in the early 1700s, the Society for the Propagation of the Gospel was founded by the religious education movement. She states: "The society was established in London in 1701 to work among blacks and Indians in the colonies. As part of the Church of England, it sent a number of clergymen to evangelize the slaves and to provide them with basic religious education. The clergy included Samuel Thomas (1702), LeJeau (1706), Ludan (1717), Gilbert Jones (1711), and Parnal (1722), whose parish had as many as 700 slaves, some of whom understood English" (Urban Education, 72). Evangelism is very important to me because the African American church must continue to seek "souls" other than those who already attend the church. The Christian education program must teach parishioners how to "go forth" and take the "Good News."

In *British Humanitarianism*, William A. Bultmann contributes a chapter, "The S.P.G. and the Foreign Settler in the American Colonies." Therein he discusses religious missions and their purpose in providing funds for those who were neglected aid. Many religious groups in the colonies had lost contact with European churches, and the Society for the Propagation of the Gospel provided assistance from funds they had recruited (51). This society was focused on helping all people, including African Americans.

### Surveys on Religious Education in the African American Church

In the early nineties, four known analyses for the African American Sunday school provided the African American church with much information about the African American Sunday school. The results are important because they provide us with firsthand knowledge: one by Scripture Press, one by Thomas Leland as a dissertation for Southern

Baptist Theological Seminary, another by Dr. Colleen Birchette and one by Dr. Oneal Sandidge. The first two sent out questionnaires to African American churches from mailing lists. In *Urban Church Education*, Colleen Birchette in her chapter "A History of Religious Education in the Black Church" writes: "Scripture Press sent out 5,110 questionnaires and got back 195 (3.8 percent response rate). Leland sent out 347 and got back 66 (19 percent response rate)" (79-80). In 1986, Dr. Birchette conducted a study for Urban Ministries with segments dealing with religious education.

The more recent of the four, a survey was conducted by Dr. Oneal C. Sandidge, while a doctoral student at Drew University Theological Seminary in 1990-91. The results were in a published dissertation May 1992. Dr. Sandidge, assisted by church members from Nathalie, Virginia, of New Second Buffalo Baptist Church and assistant Rev. Ronnie Clark, conducted a survey by visiting various national African American denominational conventions in 1981-82, speaking to denominations about his doctoral thesis and the need for knowing what's happening in the African American church school. The survey was tallied by David C. Cook Publishing Company. A total of 1,500 surveys were given out. Four hundred and forty-three surveys were fully completed and tallied. Ninety-four came out of the Progressive Convention; 54 from National Baptist, U.S.A.; 95 National Missionary Baptist of America; 13 African American Episcopal (by mail); 112 African Methodist Episcopal Zion (A.M.E.Z.); and 75 Urban Ministry (Christian Education Convention). In addition, Oneal C. Sandidge established a select committee at New Second Buffalo Baptist Church to meet with six major African American denominational select church representatives to evaluate Sunday school literature in the African American church. The information is available in the doctoral dissertation through national dissertation abstracts.

## Many Denominations Played a Role in the Shaping of the African American Sunday Church School

There are many denominations that can attest to their Sunday school origins. For the purpose of this study, the Baptists, Methodists and Presbyterians are studied. This does not limit nor disqualify other denominations from being a part of the origins of the African American

Sunday school. These denominations studied do show some of the earliest origins for the African American Sunday school.

## Baptists

Various African American Baptist churches played important roles in the organizing of the African American Sunday school. In *Black Firsts—2,000 Years of Extraordinary Achievement*, the first known Black Baptist was Quassey, a member of the Newton, Rhode Island Church. In *The Rise of Religious Education*, James Tyms states:

> The role played by Baptists in the development of the modern Sunday school has been noted. The school, started in Pawtucket in 1797, is reported to have grown out of the suggestions made by David Benedict, the influence of which is believed to have been the motivating force in the establishment of the first country Sunday school at West Dedham, Massachusetts, by Mrs. Betsy Baker in 1817. Mrs. Baker had formerly lived in Rhode Island and had probably learned something of the Slater Sunday School. (118)

Most churches were organized before the Sunday school. However, groups met in various locations for teachings before the church service to establish the Sunday school. According to general history about Black churches, the Silver Bluff Baptist Church in Beach Island, South Carolina (first noted African American church); the First African Baptist Church (known as the first Colored Baptist church, the oldest African American church because the original Silver Bluff does not exist) in Savannah, Georgia; The First Baptist Church in Petersburg, Virginia; the Gillfield Baptist Church in Petersburg, Virginia; and Congdon Baptist Church in Providence, Rhode Island are considered early African American churches.

In an interview with a church historian, Deacon Harry James of First African Baptist Church in Savannah, Georgia, the Silver Bluff Baptist Church in South Carolina operated from 1773-78. In his opinion, the present Silver Bluff Baptist Church had been formed by some concerned persons but is not an extension of the original because no record is found of a legal extension. In other words, the present Silver Bluff Baptist Church might not have anything to do with the original Silver Bluff Baptist Church.

In 1788, the history of the First African Baptist Church in Savannah, Georgia reminds us that Andrew Bryan founded the oldest

African American church, the First Colored Baptist Church now known as the First African Baptist Church on Montgomery Street in Savannah, Georgia. When asked about the Sunday school, Historian Harry James provides the following:

> In the year 1826 the first Negro Sunday School in North America was started in this church (First African Baptist Church). The initiative was taken by the independent Presbyterian church whose superintendent, Mr. Lowell Mason, appointed Mr. George W. Coe, Mr. John Lewis, and Mr. James Barr to undertake the work with the colored people in the First African Baptist Church. Mr. Coe was the superintendent until his death when he was succeeded by a Mr. William Bee. The average attendance of this school was about two hundred. Sometimes they were divided into classes and then at times the superintendent gave instruction from the desk. Special emphasis was upon behavior and obedience. Each scholar was asked to bring their masters a certificate of good behavior for the week. Those who were fortunate to have such certificate were made to stand that they might be complimented before the school and inspire others to follow their example. As a token, they were given a ticket with a Scripture text. Those reported as having been bad during the week were made to stand also to blush in shame and, perhaps, receive a reprimand. These white brethren presided over the Sunday school until December 27, 1835. After that date the church maintained the school with great success. (Independent Presbyterian records provided by Historian Deacon Harry James.)

The First Baptist Church in Petersburg, Virginia also has a great history. In their history brochure entitled "Celebrating More than 200 Years of Christian Witness," some claim that First Baptist Church in Petersburg, Virginia is the first African American church; however, the charter has not been located to verify this date. Until the date is verified, Silver Bluff remains the first known chartered African American church. According to this brochure their church was founded in 1756 and organized in 1774. The brochure further reads:

> In 1758 and 1759 arrangements were made to organize the members into a church; however, they remained scattered until 1774 when Rev. John Michaels united them and formed a regular Baptist church known as the First African Baptist Church on the estate of Col. William Byrd. This organization was moved to Petersburg after the building was destroyed by fire. A house of worship was built on Harrison Street near the present location. Elder John Benn was pastor at that time.

According to a document entitled "Some interesting accounts of the Sunday school of the First Baptist Church," "Their Sunday school was established in April 1865 by Deacon Spencer Green immediately after the Emancipation. He also established a Sunday school in 1874 in Bland-ford. Approximately in 1884, 200 pupils and ten teachers were at the Bland-ford school. He served until 1891."

Another historic church is the Gillfield Baptist Church. In an interview with and written statement by pastor Dr. Grady Powell:

> This church was founded in 1786 and its founding date of 1788 as a Davenport Port Church in 1788. In 1797, the church became an autonomous institution, yet having a mixed congregation. It was all African American in the early 1800s when its name became Sandy Beach Baptist Church. Then, before 1818 the church was moved to Collier's Alley and changed its name to the Church of the Lord Jesus Christ. In 1818, the church's name was changed again to Gillfield Baptist Church and moved to Farmer and Perry Streets in Petersburg, Virginia. The Sunday school was formed in 1803.

Another resource provides that another Sunday school was formed before 1803. In *The Rise of Religious Education Among Negro Baptists*, James Tyms states in his chapter "The Sunday School Movement," "early types of modern Sunday schools began in 1785. The claim of who actually began the first Sunday school remains unknown (115). He also elaborates since 1785, William Elliot has been known for starting the first American Sunday school in his home near Bradford's Neck, Accomac County, Virginia. Bishop Ashbury was also in charge of the organization of a Sunday school that originated in the home of Thomas Crenshaw in Hanover, Virginia in 1786. In 1791, poor children were afforded religious Sunday instruction through the First-Day or Sunday School Society. Then, in 1793, Katy Ferguson, a colored woman of New York city, began a Sunday school (116).

In addition, James Tyms informs us that Boston was known for initiating a Sunday school in 1791. In 1794, a Sunday school got started in Paterson, New Jersey. In 1797, Samuel Slater and David Benedict supported a Sunday school in Pawtucket, Rhode Island. Pittsburgh had a beginning of a school in 1800 (116).

Tyms also states that early Baptist Sunday schools for Negroes were organized for religious instruction. He adds:

> It was organized solely for religious instruction, a purpose which

makes it different from all other schools then in existence. There seems to be no particular reference to Negroes being in the schools listed here. But there are suggestions—the Negro was largely a member of the white churches and his plight was a motivating factor among those who desired to aid his growth and development. He was probably a member of the Sunday school organized in Philadelphia in 1815. For in this city three ladies of the First Baptist Church began a Sunday school movement which had its aims and interest in children of poverty, ignorance, and degradation. There were few Sunday schools among Negroes before 1865. (118-119)

In *The Baptists*, William Henry Brackney points to the fact that Mary Webb in Boston united in 1798 with a Baptist congregation and became baptized by immersion. She worked with women societies for missionaries purposes and helped in distributing Bibles and influencing groups to assist with the organization of Sunday schools (279-280).

In addition to the references cited, another resource provides much insights for us. In *A History of Black Baptists*, Leroy Fitts provides information about a school for African Americans. In 1815, Deacon William Crane, a white leather merchant and member of the First Baptist Church, Richmond, Virginia organized a school for African Americans in the First African Baptist Church (52). A slave, Moses Clayton, attended the school. Around 1834, Moses C. Clayton arrived in Baltimore and used an old schoolhouse on Young and Thompson Streets as a Sunday school (53). Then in 1836, Moses C. Clayton organized his separate black Baptist church (53).

In a telephone interview in 1993, Historian Stanley Lemons of First Baptist Church in Providence, Rhode Island states that George Willis, an African American, established the African Union Meeting and School House Society in 1819/1820. Sunday school was taught to African Americans during this period. The society split in three groups in the 1830s: Free Will Baptists, Methodists, and the leftovers composed of seven men and two women met to form the Meeting Street Baptist Church.

In another telephone interview in 1993, Dr. Robert Carter, pastor of Congdon Baptist Church in Providence, provided in a conversation that the Meeting Street Baptist Church moved to Congdon Street and became the Congdon Street Baptist Church in 1875, the oldest African American Church in Rhode Island. It is said that Sunday school was also taught in 1815 by a white woman, Maria Gano, on Olney Street, whose father was pastor of the white First Baptist Church, Providence, Rhode Island. In 1818, this Sunday school leader met in Dr. Gano's study to create a Union Sunday school for both white and African Americans.

## Methodists

The Methodists played an important role in the shaping of the African American Sunday school. Comments will be made about various Methodist denominations. In *The Big Little School*, Robert Lynn and Elliott Wright remind us about a Methodist who helped shaped the Sunday school. Hannah Ball, a pious Methodist, gathered the "wild little company" in her home for Sunday instruction as early as 1763 (3).

In a directory on African American religious bodies, published by Howard University, Dr. Calvin Morris states that Methodism was introduced in the United States in 1766 from England by Charles and John Wesley and their associates (238). Calvin Morris further shows that there are many Methodists: Union American Methodist Episcopal Church, Inc., African Union First Colored Methodist Protestant Church, African Methodist Episcopal Church, African Methodist Episcopal Zion Church, Christian Methodist Episcopal Church, Free Christian Zion Church of Christ, Reformed Methodist Union Episcopal Church, and Wesleyan Methodist Church of America. In spite of the number of Methodist denominations, this book highlights the Sunday schools in the African Methodist Episcopal Church, the African Methodist Episcopal Zion, and the Christian Methodist Episcopal Church.

In *The History of the A. M. E. Church*, Daniel Payne states that Sabbath Schools were progressing in 1845. He cites in Baltimore a flourishing Sunday school where 318 scholars, one common school and missionary society had been formed (182-83).

Daniel Payne then states that the A. M. E. is noted for its Sunday school beginnings. He writes:

> In this respect the Sunday schools in America were but following the pattern set in England a few years earlier. The founding of the movement there, about 1780, was the work of a Christian newspaper editor, Robert Raikes.... In America too the Methodists have claimed the first Sunday school. William Elliott, a Methodist layman, began in 1785 to instruct his own children and several young

men "bound out" to him in his own home in Virginia. He also instructed slaves at another hour... another Virginia Methodist has been credited with the first American Sunday school. According to the first report of the Methodist Sunday School Union, the first Sunday school in America was conducted by Thomas Crenshaw in 1786 (273-74).

It is my view that slaves did not attend many of these schools. They were sponsored by masters and many of the masters closed doors to African Americans. African Americans had already created their own Sunday schools in homes when masters prevented them to worship prior to the masters creating their own Sunday schools. This thought will remind us that African Americans were well awake in the formation of the Sunday school.

Dr. Dennis Dickerson, Historiographer for the A.M.E. in Williamstown, Massachusetts, confirms the African Methodist Episcopal Church as formally becoming a denomination in 1816 and likely the Sunday school started in one of the oldest churches, e.g. Mother Bethel in Philadelphia, Bethel in Baltimore, or New York City.

In *Christian Education Journey of Black Americans—Past, Present, Future*, Grant Shockley provides that Richard Allen, the founder and first Bishop of the African Methodist Episcopal Church, established in 1816, organized the first black church-related school in America for the Methodist Episcopal Church. The Sunday School Union was organized in 1882 by Charles S. Smith. In 1888, Charles S. Smith became the first black Christian education expert as Corresponding Secretary of the Union. Then in 1874, William Coleman conducted the first Black Leadership Training Enterprise. In 1823, in Salem, North Carolina, African Americans attended "black chapel" and Sunday school built for them (12). In *African Methodism in the South—Twenty Five Years of Freedom*, Rev. Wesley Gaines speaks about A.M.E. Sunday schools. He comments: " The Sunday school becomes a family, with strong family relations and ties" (60).

## The African Methodist Episcopal Zion Church

According to history, the A. M. E. Z. Church was founded in New York in 1800 and included a school room. It appears that the A. M. E. Z. Church was active in education for African Americans.

In *Christian Education Journey of Black American—Past, Present, Future*, Grant Shockley reminds us that Sunday school work was organized in this denomination a generation prior to the Civil War, along the east and far west at Pittsburgh (12).

## The Christian Methodist Episcopal Church

Grant Shockley also informs us that in 1870, the Colored "Christian" Methodist Church had Sunday schools prior to their established denomination. Sunday schools were not organized into a department until 1918. In 1934, the department was formed with other departments to create the General Board of Religious Education. In 1950, the General Conference Board of Education merged with the Board of Religious Education to form the General Board of Christian Education. He goes on to say: "The curriculum materials used in the C.M.E. Church are adapted versions of the materials of the United Methodist Church" (C. E. Journey, 13).

In addition to Baptists and Methodists origins of the African American Sunday schools, Presbyterians also had interesting origins.

## Presbyterians

In *Urban Church Education*, Colleen Birchette discusses in her article "A History of Religious Education in the Black Church" that as early as 1747, Virginia Presbyterians made some efforts toward religious education through the ministries of John Todd and Samuel Davies to instruct blacks. Samuel Davies and John Todd reported baptizing and ministering to 300 persons (73). In *A Brief History of the Presbyterians*, Lefferts Loetcher informs us that the permanent organization of Presbyterians in America did not form a permanent presbytery until late 1706. Before this time, many Presbyterian congregations existed (50). He then states that there were two groups, the Lutherans (Martin Luther) and the Reformed, implying the reformed or Presbyterians (John Calvin), which had a split because of issues such as the Lord's Supper. He did not mention about the Sunday church school (22).

## The Role of Conventions in Confirming African American Sunday Church Schools

Some churches started their own Sunday school; of course, we have no record for many beginnings. After Sunday schools were organized, many conventions (type of a denominational affiliation) went forth to produce publishing boards or to recommend publishing boards for Sunday school literature. Be reminded, when conventions were organized, Sunday schools were already in operation. For example, according to a brochure "Black Baptists in America and the Origins of their Conventions," Sloan S. Hodges lists a number of national organizations and their origin dates such as 1840—American Baptist Missionary Convention in New York, 1864—The Western and Southern Missionary Baptist Convention, 1866—The Consolidated American Baptist Missionary Convention organized in Richmond, Virginia, 1866—The American National Convention was born, 1893—The National Baptist Educational Convention, 1895—The National Baptist Convention, USA, Inc., 1897—The Lott Carey Foreign Mission Convention, 1915—The National Baptist Convention of America, unincorporated, 1916—The Progressive National Baptist Convention, Inc.

## A Great Pioneer and Mother of the African American Sunday School

*Who is the greatest African American pioneer in the African American Sunday school? The African American Sunday school was not founded by whites. It was founded by African Americans, with the woman Katie Ferguson as its most noted pioneer.*

Katie Ferguson (some spell her name Katy) is the most noted person for organizing the African American Sunday school in 1793. She is the most noted because of her documented records. We then should consider Katie Ferguson as a founder of the African American Sunday school. This does not imply that others did not shape the African American Sunday school nor that other unknown contributors did not exist.

Since Katie is African American, African Americans should respect her efforts for the African American church. Prior efforts are helpful to us, but Katie's efforts are most likely the most understood, documented history and the most reliable source for our historical study. Prior ministries existed, as noted, but few details are known about them. Katie was a member of Second Presbyterian Church in New York and was very devoted to her work. A brochure entitled "Please Count Me in Too" provides that her home is known as Katy Ferguson House, 162 West 130th Street in New York City. The brochure also states, "These babies at the Katy Ferguson House must have help if they are to grow into healthy, happy boys and girls." A pastor of Second Presbyterian Church was interviewed by phone in 1990. He stated that he did recall the name Katie Ferguson. The pastor of Second Presbyterian stated that he had tried numerous times to locate written documents about Katie. He wrote to pastors, but received little information. Katie was likely the daughter of a slave since her mother either died or was taken captive by slave owners. Katie went to New York in the 1780s where she taught math and reading during the week. Katie was said to have an humble spirit which caused her to encourage others to do Christian work. Katie broke tradition at the Second Presbyterian Church by leaving the balcony area where blacks sat and came to the altar to personally receive Holy Communion.

In *Eminent Americans*, Benson Lossing discusses Katy. "Katy was a colored woman, born a slave while her mother was on her passage from Virginia to New York.... When Katy was eight years of age, her mother was sold, and they never met again. Her own anguish taught her to sympathize with desolate children, and they became the great care of her life" ( 404).

In *Cubberleys History of Education*, Hallie Q. Brown in "Homespun Heroines and Other Women of Distinction" also discusses Katy Ferguson. She comments: "Katy Ferguson with no knowledge of Raikes' movement, with scant material, and with no preparation save her piety and her warm mother's heart, gave to New York City its first Sunday school" (3).

In addition, in *The Narratives of Colored Americans*, E. Mott states: "She lived in a part of the city where there were many poor families, and many of both colored and white children who had none to care for their bodies or souls" (66-67).

Excerpts from a Children's Day sermon by the Reverend L. Humphrey Walz at Second Presbyterian Church discusses Katy Ferguson. He states: "Ours is the oldest Sunday school in New York because some folk looked on a little colored girl named Katy Ferguson, in the spirit of Jesus Christ and because when she herself grew up, she looked on children in the same spirit" (Second Presbyterian Church).

## The Press and Katie Ferguson

According to an undated New York press release written by Second Presbyterian Church:

> Katy Ferguson, a former slave who dedicated herself to working with children, will be honored by a cantata "All Is Well," that will receive its premiere performance as part of a special vesper service on All Saints Day, November 1 at 4 p.m. at Second Presbyterian Church. " 'All Is Well' are the last words of Katy Ferguson," said Rev. Wilson; they seem a fitting title to a work meant to 'raise up' this slightly-known saint. She is thought to have begun the first Sabbath Day Schools in the city in the 1790s. She personally took 48 children, 20 of them white, until she could find homes for them (Katie taught these children the Bible).
>
> Although she was a slave, the people of Second Church (then called "The Scotch Church") helped her purchase her freedom and establish a livelihood. She was well-known for the cakes and confections and for her talent with lace. She died, probably of cholera, in 1854.

Another news press, **Philadelphia Tribune, June 7, 1947** discussed Katy.

> Miss Katy Ferguson, one of America's pioneers in the field of education will be honored at the Children's Day service at Second Presbyterian Church, 6 West 96th Street, New York, this coming Sunday morning, June 8th at 11 a.m. The first Negro to be received into the membership of that church, she more than justified the hospitality afforded her when she established there in 1793 the first Sunday school in the city.

Then a press, **New York Times, June 7, 1947** states:

> The Children's Day service at the Second Presbyterian Church, 6 West Ninety-Sixth Street, honored Katy Ferguson, the first Negro to be received into the membership in the church and who established there in 1793, the first Sunday school in the city.
>
> The Rev. L. Humphrey Walz, the pastor said in his sermon, "Ours is the oldest Sunday school in New York, because some folk looked on a little child, a little colored girl named Katy Ferguson, in the spirit of Jesus Christ and because when she herself grew up she looked on children in the same spirit."

In Ohio, the **Cincinnati News Press, June 5, 1947** states:

> The First Negro to be received into membership of that church (Second Presbyterian), she more than justified the hospitality afforded her when she established there in 1793 the first Sunday school in the city... Her influence in the field of child welfare and adult education as well as the example of the happy cooperation between members of different races, she and her colleagues afforded, will be highlighted in the sermon of Rev. L. Humphrey Waltz, the present pastor.

In New York, **The New York Amsterdam News, June 21, 1947** notes:

> When Katy was sixteen, a Scotch woman, Mrs. Isabella Graham, paid $200 for her freedom and helped her to go in business as a cake-baker. At eighteen, she married but soon lost her husband and two children by death. The loss of her mother and family found her alone but she gained spiritual comfort and joy helping needy children. It is said that forty-eight children were placed by her during those years. She could neither read nor write but would gather the children, Negro and white in her home on Warren Street every Sunday afternoon to recite stories of the Bible she had heard, and taught them to sing hymns and spirituals. One Sunday, Dr. John Mason found her teaching the children and invited her to bring them to church on Murray Street where she continued to teach them.... And from this beginning the Sabbath schools in the Scotch Church were started, which it is believed to have led to the establishment of Sunday schools in other churches of New York City. Katy died at age eighty of cholera.

### Summary of Leaflet on Katie Ferguson

In the brochure entitled "Katy Ferguson, a Pioneer in the Sunday School Movement," S. E. Grinstead states historical insights about Katy Ferguson that the Sunday School Publishing Board of the National Baptist Convention, U.S.A., Inc. (located in the archival division) has provided.

*(Revised quote—by permission of the Sunday School Publishing Board, National Baptist Convention, U.S.A., Inc.):*

The early beginning and development of the Sunday school work in England and in the United States of America were expressions of deep concerns for others. Among the early pioneers of the Sunday schools in the United States was Katie Ferguson, a black (African American) woman who founded the first Sunday school in New York

City. "Katie," spelled by some as "Katy," and called by others as "Catherine," was born in 1779 while her slave mother was being transported from Virginia to New York City. When Katie was four years old her mother was sold to another slave master, and she was torn away from her mother forever. However, Katie remembered that before she and her mother had parted, her mother "knelt down and laid her hand on my head and gave me to God." At the age of fifteen, Katie the orphan girl joined the Second Presbyterian Church at Cedar Street between Broadway and Nassau in New York, under their first pastor, the Rev. John Mason.

Some of the members of the church objected to having Katie sit down with them at the communion table, but Rev. Mason had them understand that "whosoever shall do the will of my Father which is in heaven, the same is my brother, sister and mother." Katie was soon an accepted member and a warm friend of many families.

The Sunday school, in Katie Ferguson's day and for some time after, was not connected with the church as we know it to be today. Katie and those who followed her example believed that even the simplest education, along with kindness and cleanliness, would help children learn other Christian virtues.

In 1814, Katie regularly gathered the children in the neighborhood into her home where she got suitable persons to come to hear them say their catechism lessons and teach them to read. It is interesting to note that Katie, herself illiterate, should be one of the early pioneers of the Sunday school. She committed much of the Bible to memory and was quite capable of hearing the children recite verses. Much of the Sunday school learning involved memorization of hymns and Scriptures. A report of 1818 indicated that of the 88 registered students, 26 were black (African American); 11 were adults. Therefore, Katie's Sunday school served whites and blacks (African Americans), children and adults.

She supported herself by making delicate confections for dinner and evening parties. She also started the first Children's Aid Society. It is stated that she picked up from the streets at different times some forty-eight orphans or destitute children; fed, clothed, and educated them to the best of her ability. It was said that every one of these children turned out well. It was stated also that, "The Sunday school was particularly helpful in the South, as it stirred the land-holding classes, much as the better-to-do classes, in the towns and cities had been stirred to do something for the education of the children of the poor. These schools, too, being open to all as well as to the poor and lowly, had small but increasing influence in leveling class distinctions and in making a Common Day School seem possible."

Katie Ferguson's "School for the Poor" was followed by an organization of New York women for the extension of secular instruction among the poor. Ellwood P. Cubberly in *Public Education in the United States,* commenting on this relationship, stated that in 1797 Samuel Slaters' Factory School was opened at Pawtucket, Rhode Island. Other cities opening Sunday schools were Boston, Pittsburgh, Patterson, Jersey City, and Portsmouth.

Though the Sunday school may not be said to have substituted for the common school, it can be justly claimed to have played a peculiarly significant part in the development of the free school idea as modern society has evolved it. It helped to establish a new relationship between the rich and the poor. Sunday school teaching from the beginning was aimed at meeting the needs of learners: the underprivileged. The needs of the underprivileged who were left without educational opportunity to learn the fundamentals of reading. The needs of the poor children of the streets to learn hygiene, discipline, and social graces were important parts of their Sunday school curriculum.

We are indebted to Katie Ferguson and other early pioneers of the Sunday School Movement. The pupil still occupies the most important place to be focused upon in the class with the understanding teacher as leader and guide. One should remember also that behind the scenes stands the organizational structure of officers and staff leaders who share with those who teach with adequate plans; the programs, and tools of learning that help to make effective instruction meet the growing needs of the total church of today (Folder by the Division of Public Relations—"Katie Ferguson, Pioneer in the Sunday School Movement").

| CHART ON SUNDAY SCHOOL HISTORICAL INFORMATION | |
|---|---|
| **Name** | **Date** |
| SILVER BLUFF BAPTIST CHURCH IN SOUTH CAROLINA | 1773 |
| William Elliot, Bradford's Neck in Accomac County, Virginia | 1785 |
| Thomas Crenshaw in Hanover, Virginia | 1786 |
| First Sunday School Society | 1791 |
| KATIE FERGUSON OF SECOND PRESBYTERIAN CHURCH IN NEW YORK, NEW YORK | 1793 |
| A Sunday School in Patterson, New Jersey | 1794 |
| Samuel Slater and David Benedict aided a Sunday School in Pawtucket, Rhode Island | 1797 |
| A Sunday School in Pittsburgh | 1800 |
| GILLFIELD BAPTIST CHURCH IN PETERSBURG, VIRGINIA | 1803 |
| Deacon William Crane (white) | 1815 |
| FIRST UNION MEETING AND SCHOOL HOUSE SOCIETY, PROVIDENCE, RHODE ISLAND | 1819/1820 |
| FIRST AFRICAN BAPTIST CHURCH IN SAVANNAH, GEORGIA | 1826 |
| A. M. E. Sunday School, Chillicothe, Ohio | 1829 |
| Moses Clayton | 1836 |
| FIRST BAPTIST CHURCH IN PETERSBURG, VIRGINIA | 1865 |

# SOURCES CITED

Birchette, Colleen "A History of Religious Education in the Black Church." in *Urban Church Education* Edited by Donald B. Rogers Birmingham: Religious Education Press, 1989.

Blackwell, John A. *The Black Church and The Black Experience*. Nashville: United Methodist Publishing House, 1971.

Boylan, Anne M. *Sunday School—The Formation of An American Institution, 1790-1880*. New Haven: Yale University Press, 1988.

Brackney, William Henry. *The Baptists*. New York: Greenwood Press, 1988.

Brown, Hallie Q. "Homespun Heroines and Other Women of Distinction" in *Cubberly's History of Education*. Xenia, Ohio: Aldine Publishing Company, 1922.

Brown, Lorenzo Quincy. "The Study of the Sunday School—Provided for the Immediate Department of the Colored Methodist Episcopal Church," Thesis Howard University, June 1940, pp1-4.

Bucke, Emory Stevens, editor. *The History of American Methodism*, Vol.1. Nashville: Abingdon Press, 1964.

Bultmann, William A. *British Humanitarianism*. Edited by Samuel McCulloch. New York: the Church Historical Society, 1950.

Dickerson, Dennis, Historiographer for A.M.E. Williamstown, Massachusetts, telephone and written communication, March 26, 1993.

First Baptist Church—Brochure—"Celebrating More Than 200 Years of Christian Witness."

——————— Brochure—"Some Interesting Accounts of the Sunday School of the First Baptist Church."

Fitts, Leroy. *A History of Black Baptists*. Nashville: Broadman Press, 1985.

Franklin, John Hope and Alfred A. Moss, Jr. "The Effort to Attain Peace" in *From Slavery to Freedom—A History of African Americans*, seventh edition. New York: McGraw-Hill, Inc., 1994.

Gaines, Wesley. *African Methodism in the South*. Atlanta: Franklin Publishing House,1890.

Greene, Lorenzo J. *Working with Carter G. Woodson—The Father of Black History—A Diary of 1928-1930*. Baton Rouge: Louisiana State University Press, 1989.

Grinstead, S. E., Sr., "Katy Ferguson, Pioneer in the Sunday School Movement," Published by the Sunday School Publishing Board of the National Baptists Convention, U.S.A. Inc., Folder.

Harris, James. Independent Presbyterian Records by the First African Baptist Church. Savannah, Georgia, 1925.

Hodges, Sloan, compiler. Brochure "Black Baptists in America and The Origins of Their Conventions." D.C.: Progressive National Baptist Convention, Inc.

Howard, Phillip E. *Sunday Schools—The World Around*. The Official Report of the World's Fifth Sunday School Convention, 1907

*Joint Educational Manual—Black Perspectives in Church Education*, "Role and function of Resources."

Loetcher, Lefferts. *A Brief History of the Presbyterians*. Philadelphia: The Westminster Press, 1958.

Lossing, Benson. *Eminent Americans*. New York: Mason Brothers, 1857.

Lynn, Robert W. and Elliott Wright. *The Big Little School—Two Hundred Years of the Sunday School*. New York: Harper and Row, 1971.

Kellar, Marcel. *Building a Strong Sunday Church School*. Nashville: National Baptist Publishing Board, 1987.

Morris, Calvin. "African Americans and Methodism" in *Directory of African American Religious Bodies—A Compendium by Howard University School of Divinity*. Edited by Payne, Wardell. D.C.: Howard University Press, 1991.

Mott, E. *Narratives of Colored Americans*. New York: Bowne, 1882.

Nieman, Donald G. *To Set the Law in Motion—The Freedmen's Bureau and the Legal Rights of Blacks 1865-1868*. Millwood, New York: KTO Press, 1979.

Payne, Daniel. *History of the A.M.E. Church.* Nashville: Publishing House of the Sunday School Union, 1891.

"Please Count Me In Too"— Brochure—Katy Ferguson House.

Powell, Grady. Interview, June 10, 1993, Pastor of Gillfield Baptist Church. Petersburg. *Pulpit Helps.*16: (November 1990).

Report developed during Krisheim II Conference on Education Resources for Black Churches, August 31—September 3, 1970, sponsored by the Black Christian Education Administrative and Coordinating Committee.

Rogers, Donald B. *Urban Church Education.* Birmingham: Religious Education Press, 1989.

Rogers, Donald, *Urban Church Education.* Colleen Birchett in "History of Religious Education in the Black Church." Birmingham: Religious Education Press, 1989.

Seymour, Jack. *From Sunday School to Church School— Continuities in Protestant Church Education in the United Stated, 1860-1929.* D.C. : University Press of America, 1982.

Shipley, Anthony J. "Choosing and Using Resources in the Black Church"— Prepared by the Department of Youth Publications, Section on Curriculum Resources, Board of Discipleship of the United Methodist Church-Published by Graded Press, 1973.

Shockley, Grant S. *Christian Education Journey of Black Americans—Past, Present, Future.* Nashville: Discipleship Resources, 1985.

Smith, Jessie Carney, editor. *Black Firsts—2,000 Years of Extraordinary Achievement.* Detroit: Visible Ink Press, 1994.

Smith, Sid. *Reaching the Black Community through the Sunday School.* Nashville: Sunday School Board of Southern Baptist Church Convention, 1984.

_____. *Sunday School Growth*, Olivia Cloud. Nashville: Convention Press—The Sunday School Board of the Southern Baptist, 1990.

_____. 10 Super Sunday Schools in the Black Community.

Spencer, Ruth L. and Idris W. Jones. *The Work of the Sunday School Superintendent.* Valley Forge: Judson Press, 1994.

Stafford, Tim. "This Little Light of Mine." *Christianity Today.* (October 8, 1990).

Steward, Austin. "Termination of Slavery" in *Lift Ev'ry Voice—African American Oratory,1787-1900.* Edited by Philip S. Foner and Robert Branham. Tuscaloosa: The University of Alabama Press, 1998.

*Sunday School Informer.* (February, 1934).

Telephone conversation with Historian Stanley Lemons of First Baptist Church, Providence, Rhode Island and telephone conversation with Dr. Robert Carter, present pastor: Congdon Street Baptist Church, Providence, Rhode Island.

Telephone conversation with pastor of Second Presbyterian Church, New York, New York, Fall 1990.

Thomas, Edgar. *The First African Baptist Church in North America.*

Tyms, James. *The Rise of Religious Education Among Negro Baptists.* D.C. : University Press, 1979.

Walker, Wyatt T. "Fifth Anniversary—History Brochure" and 2/93 telephone conversation with Dr. Grady Davis and viewing the Heritage Room of Gillfield Baptist Church with Deacons Mrs. Lula E. Allgood and Mrs. Thomassine M. Burke.

Walz, L. Humphrey. "Excerpts from Sermon, June 8, 1947." Pastor of Second Presbyterian Baptist Church.

Wesley, Charles H. and Patricia Romero. *Negro Americans in the Civil War: From Slavery to Citizenship.* New York: Publishers Company, Inc. Under the Association for the Study of Negro Life and History, 1968.

Wyckoff, D. Campbell. *Renewing the Sunday School and the CCD.* Birmingham: Religious Education Press, 1986.

# CHAPTER 8

# Suggestions for African American Christian Education Programs for the Twenty-first Century

T his final chapter will remind us that we have come a long way, but we still have a long way to go. It takes all educators, pastors, and lay persons, students, and practitioners to help improve Christian education in the African American church. The African American pastor is needed to support leadership in the Department of Christian Education. He or she should place Christian education next to the pastor's budget in importance. The DCE, especially a trained DCE (seminary degree or masters in Christian/ religious education), should receive a salary comparable to one step below the pastor. The pastor can do many things to help the department. When problems arise in the direction of the DCE, the bottom line is that the pastor should assist.

I still find mega churches with no full-time DCE. Many who do have full-time directors have them working in other capacities than Christian education. The Director of Christian Education has a full-time job in guiding education in the church. Think about all the ministries that come under Christian education. This includes most of the ministries in the church, including the Sunday church school.

The African American church must understand that she does not have all the needed resources. We must share what we have with non-African Americans and vice versa. At some point all educators, regardless of race, need to come to the table to express and share concerns and information. Even non-African American churches can learn a valuable lesson from the African American church and vice versa. I suggest that seminaries seek all graduates in Christian education, inviting them to come and discuss current trends in Christian education. I think it is wise for each race to meet with their own group to pinpoint concerns. Then races may come together in a joint meeting to discuss possibilities. African American Christian educators must form a national group to assist in the church. Once trained persons come together, they can suggest ways to contact all churches and invite all Christian educators.

We are living in a time where the African American church will see more and more non-African Americans attending their churches and programs. We must not only concentrate on our priority, African American needs, but learn how to incorporate meeting the needs of non-African Americans as well. Such challenging moments are important for the African American church in considering the needs of all parishioners.

We must share resources among our own African American churches. Some leaders refuse to return telephone calls or discuss what they are doing because they are caught up in their own selves, and their own programs. This is God's program, however, and we should be striving toward the same purpose: to learn how to prepare for our new home, heaven. In addition, directors must learn to use modern technology. We need to train parishioners how to use the computer and to take advantage of the programs that will help us learn more about Christian education. We must go into the community and work with community leaders to learn how we can help each other. Both the community and the church should consider joint workshops to educate the community. The church should be the focal point of the whole community. The African American church should concentrate on learning how to greet visitors, how to show love to visitors and members, and to make all people, regardless of their background or lifestyle, feel and know that God is the God who can bring about change.

The church can no longer think that leaders and teachers should not be evaluated. Some evaluating tool should be in place. Usually the DCE is responsible for this job. This means that the volunteer and paid persons should be evaluated. Hopefully, the church will move toward creating a budget for more paid positions and delete some of the volunteer positions. In most cases, when one is paid, he or she will show more promising work for the job. In other cases, some volunteers work harder than paid persons.

Christian education is no joke for the church. We need to include all parishioners in this work. It is now time to have more programs for our senior citizens and little children. Some churches concentrate on the Sunday school and youth departments. We also need to share more education about ministries such as dance, theater, and African experiences to provide a wholesome program in the African American church. As we think about ministries, it is important to think about family worship. The family needs a time, perhaps once a month, to come to church, sit together, and recall family values.

Every African American church should consider developing a manual for its Department of Christian Education and later expanding that manual into handbooks for each ministry, including the Sunday church school. The curriculum must be determined according to the needs of students.

Lastly, the church must establish and seek more than one day a week to have Bible study. Some churches have Bible study after the morning worship and twice during the week to meet the needs of those who are working and cannot attend one standard Bible class. In addition, classes must be interesting and appealing to all ages. The teacher should consider supplementary materials when planning for these studies. Churches should also consider Home Bible Studies for those who cannot attend the church.

In summary, the African American church has really made progress through the years. It is my prayer that we will continue to progress and to uplift the work of Christ!

*Should you desire me for a workshop or preaching: Contact me at: 4752 Elon Road, Monroe, Virginia 24574, and your invitation will be forwarded to me. I also serve as a consultant. If you have needs to modify or start a new Christian education program, you may also contact me to work with your church for a short or long period of time.*

*Rev. Dr. Oneal Sandidge*

# *Appendixes*

**All Forms Are Only Suggested Forms for Your Ministry**

## Appendix 1

## Sample Job Descriptions

### Job Title: DIRECTOR OF CHRISTIAN EDUCATION

**Job Description:** The DCE is responsible for the entire educational ministry and all teaching that takes place in the church.

### Responsibilities

The DCE will:

1. be an ex-officio to the Board of Christian Education or Christian Education Committee offering assistance, guidance, and direction in the planning, implementation, coordination and evaluation of the entire church program of Christian education, including all teaching ministries, and any other ministries that teach; e.g., the Sunday church school.
2. review and approve the Bible Study Programs, including VBS.
3. supervise all ministries, leaders, workers and programs under the Board of Christian Education.
4. serve as the administrative network for Christian education in the church.
5. evaluate the entire Christian staff (leaders and teachers) and make recommendations to the Board of Christian Education and to the Pastor.
6. review all workshop titles, speakers, activities and curriculum content.
7. have an option to attend Board meetings
8. report directly to the pastor.
9. recommend a budget for the Board of Christian Education.

## Job Title: DIRECTOR OF MINISTRY, e.g., Director of Youth/Children

Some churches have a paid position known as " Director" for some ministries. In the case of such position, the following is suggested:

**Job Description:** The Director is responsible for guiding the department leaders and for monitoring the entire program, including curriculum.

### Responsibilities

The Director will:
1. evaluate ministry needs.
2. coordinate ministry plans with department leader.
3. serve as an advisor to the department leader, ministry leaders, ministry workers, and attendees.
4. develop or modify, if need exists, a curriculum for the ministry in consultation and with approval from the DCE.
5. consult community and national churches and church leaders of a similar ministry to review their curriculum for fresh ideas.
6. negotiate work hours with the DCE. This may include attending some ministry meetings and board meetings and other after-hour events.
7. work with the team ministry to provide a wholesome ministry.
8. attend Board meetings.
9. seek continuing education.
10. report to the DCE.

## Job Title: DEPARTMENT LEADERS

**Job Description:** Department leaders are responsible for guiding the entire ministry, all teachers, ministry leaders and ministry workers, ministry participants and learning experiences. If a director is employed, duties may diminish.

### Responsibilities

The department leader will:
1. attend Board meetings.
2. be responsible to monitor ministry meetings and all learning experiences.

3. survey parishioners at least once a year to learn of ministry needs.
4. survey ministry leaders and workers at least once a year.
5. survey ministry attendees at least once a year.
6. follow the ministry calendar.
7. report to the director of the ministry or to the DCE if no director.

## Job Title: MINISTRY LEADERS

**Job Description:** To lead ministry meetings in conjunction with the department leader and department workers. Carry out plans of the department leader/director.

Ministry leaders may be allocated certain areas of responsibilities for the ministry, e.g., in charge of Bible study or activities. Ministry leaders may suggest a ministry agenda to the department leader, who in turn will have an approval from the director, if such exists, and the DCE.

### Responsibilities
The ministry leader will:
1. be responsible for the assigned area(s) of ministry.
2. be in prayer for the ministry.
3. do his or her best to religiously educate ministry attendees.
4. meet with the department leader to plan and implement ministry ideas.
5. assist in all ministry activities, trips, workshops, and ministry events.
6. report to the department leader and be responsible to the director, and DCE.

## Job Title: CHAIR OF CHRISTIAN EDUCATION

**Job Description:** Coordinate activities of the Board of Christian Education. Assist in planning and executing Board activities and programs.

### Responsibilities
The Chair of the Board of Christian Education will:
1. direct, coordinate, guide and supervise Board affairs, including Board meetings.

2. serve as a representative of the Board of Christian Education.
3. serve as a resource person to the Board.
4. remind Board members to adhere to church policies, the pastor and the DCE's guidelines.
5. maintain the Board of Christian Education annual calendar.
6. assist in evaluations, training, visiting ministries and other needed Board functions, upon the request of the DCE.
7. lead Board meetings per the request of the DCE.
8. suggest and submit for approval a Board's agenda weeks prior to Board's meeting date.
9. report to the church and the DCE.

In the absence of the Chair and per sufficient notice from the Chair, the Vice-Chair will assume the responsibility of the Chair and assist in any way to carry out Board activities.

## Job Title: BOARD SECRETARY

**Job Description:** Work closely with the DCE, Chair and Vice-Chair of the Board of Christian Education in the communication and the documentation of all Board meetings and activities.

**Reports to:** DCE

**Responsibilities**
The Secretary of the Board of Christian Education will:
1. attend regular Board meetings.
2. write minutes at Board meetings and submit to Chair and DCE within two weeks notice.
3. file and maintain up-to-date rosters of all Board members, including names, addresses, telephone and fax numbers.
4. remind leaders of Board meetings and send any other correspondences upon request.
5. be responsible for all bulletins and announcements.
6. report to the Chair of the Board and the DCE.

In absence of the secretary, a volunteer may serve unless an assistant has been named.

# JOB DESCRIPTIONS FOR
# THE SUNDAY CHURCH SCHOOL

## Job Title: GENERAL SUPERINTENDENT OF THE SUNDAY CHURCH SCHOOL

**Job Description:** The General Superintendent will advise department superintendents, teachers, and assistants for Sunday church school programs, teacher training, and church school statistics, and distributing curriculum materials.

### Responsibilities
The General Superintendent will:
1. maintain Sunday school class and teacher rosters and records of all church school activities and provide copies to the DCE.
2. provide assessments and any final analysis of the Sunday church school.
3. seek ideas to enhance the Sunday church school.
4. plan proposed annual objectives and goals for the Sunday church school and submit for DCE's approval.
5. propose an annual budget for the Sunday church school and submit for DCE's consideration.
6. meet with Assistant General Superintendents and Department Superintendents to plan Sunday church school administration and to discuss all Sunday church school concerns, e.g., supplies, classroom and instruction concerns, and teacher/student concerns.
7. plan and submit to the DCE an annual calendar for consideration.
8. attend Board meetings.
9. order materials in conjunction and approval from the DCE.
10. report to the DCE.

## Job Title: SUNDAY CHURCH SCHOOL TEACHERS

**Job Description:** Sunday church school teachers will teach the Word of God.

### Responsibilities
Teachers will:
1. be born again Christians who understand the doctrines of the church.

2. spend time in daily prayer and devotions and pray for students.
3. read and study God's Word daily/weekly.
4. have a burning desire to teach.
5. be responsible for a decorative room.
6. maintain attendance and inquire about those who frequently miss class.
7. attend teachers' meetings.
8. attend in-service training.
9. up-date certification by enrolling in new phases of prospective teacher training.
10. be willing to modify teaching methods and learn new ideas.
11. use the materials set forth by the Sunday church school, including Bible version, Sunday school lessons.
12. adhere to the doctrine of the church.
13. not allow personal views to interrupt the teaching/learning process.
14. prepare lesson plans as recommended.
15. be on time for classes.
16. report to the Department Superintendent and also responsible to the General Superintendent and the DCE.

Note: Assistant teachers will only serve as teacher when they are scheduled. At no time should two teachers be in charge of a classroom. One might be an assistant, but only one teacher because students should not become confused with instruction.


## SUNDAY CHURCH SCHOOL SUPPORT STAFF

## DEPARTMENT SECRETARIES

### Department Secretaries will:
1. be responsible to the Sunday church school General Superintendent and the DCE.
2. maintain attendance and offering records for the church school department.
3. collect Sunday church school offerings.
4. maintain department attendance and offering records.
5. submit attendance/offering envelopes to church clerk.

## CLASS SECRETARIES/ASSISTANT SECRETARIES

### Class Secretaries/Assistant Secretaries
1. record class attendance and collect class offering. Record both on attendance/offering sheet in provided envelopes.
2. deliver attendance/offering envelopes to the department secretaries. *
3. maintain and periodically update current class rosters.
4. contact students who are regularly absent from class.
5. report students who are sick and shut-in, hospitalizations or deaths in immediate families.

* Adult Department Secretaries deliver attendance/offering envelopes to class secretaries in sanctuary.


## LIBRARIAN/ASSISTANT LIBRARIAN

### Librarian/Assistant Librarian
1. periodically suggest supplementary instructional materials for Sunday school classes.
2. organize Sunday school materials for each class.
3. arrange for distributing Sunday school material.

### Job Title: SUNDAY CHURCH SCHOOL STATISTICIAN

**Job Description:** Collect and prepare Sunday church school enrollment (students and teachers), attendance, and new member statistical reports. Job involves collecting Sunday church school class rosters, attendance records, and class and department secretary records to develop teacher, student and class attendance/enrollment statistics. Work closely with the church clerk and the General Superintendent of the Sunday church school. Assist in suggesting goals and objectives for the Sunday church school.

### Responsibilities
The Sunday Church School Statistician will:
1. collect and update Sunday church school class rosters from Sunday school teachers.
2. collect Sunday church attendance records from Church Clerk

weekly and prepare Sunday church school attendance statistical spreadsheet reports at least quarterly.
3. collect enrollment forms for new Sunday school students.
4. report to the General Superintendent and the DCE.

## Job Title: VACATION BIBLE SCHOOL (VBS) COORDINATOR

**Job Description**: The Coordinator will plan, train, implement, and supervise the Summer Vacation Bible School (VBS) program. The VBS program will include Bible study, Bible craft-making, field trips, community evangelism, and other creative activities.

### Responsibilities
The VBS Coordinator will:
1. prepare a proposed plan of the VBS curriculum in conjunction with the General Superintendent of the Sunday school and submit to the DCE for approval.
2. suggest VBS materials and promotional materials to the General Superintendent and DCE.
3. suggest VBS training for VBS teachers and staff to the General Superintedent and the DCE.
4. coordinate and supervise VBS classes and activities and prepare a final summary for the General Superintendent and the DCE.
5. suggest a meal menu for VBS attendees to the General Superintendent and the DCE.
6. make arrangement for all scheduled VBS field trips, approved by General Superintendent and the DCE.
8. report to the General Superintendent and the DCE.


## SOME SUGGESTED MINISTRY RESPONSIBILITIES

## Job Title: BASIC MEMBERSHIP DEPARTMENT

### Responsibilities
The Department will:
1. monitor attendance and spiritual growth for new and present members.
2. suggest yearly surveys to determine the effectiveness of the department.

3. develop and suggest goals and objectives for the Basic Membership Department.
4. meet with all sub-ministry leaders in the department to guide the various ministries.
5. serve as a caring ministry to make all members feel a part of the church.

## SAMPLE MINISTRIES UNDER THE DEPARTMENT OF BASIC MEMBERSHIP

**Job Title**: NEW MEMBER ORIENTATION MINISTRY

**Job Description**: Provide new member orientation classes for children and adults. These classes will orient members to the church and to biblical doctrine, church doctrine and denominational doctrine. There should be a separate orientation for children.

**Job Title: EXTENDED ORIENTATION FOR CHILDREN**

**Job Description:** A series of extended instruction should be planned. One might have twelve, more or less, weeks of intense instruction on many of the areas initiated in the new member orientation classes.

**Job Title: BIG BROTHER, BIG SISTER MINISTRY**

**Job Description**: This ministry will assist new members in becoming more comfortable in the church and more familiar with the congregation by teaming them with long time, saved members. This ministry will serve as a big brother and a big sister to help those in distress, to have fun, to cry and in summary, to bear one another's burden. This will mean a team for praying, concern about church attendance and to be a good listener. Friendship beyond this should not be the focus.

**Job Title: LAY PARTICIPATION MINISTRY**

**Job Description:** The Lay Participation Ministry will suggest assignment for worship/pulpit responsibilities. The pastor has the final word, unless he provides the DCE with such authority. This ministry will train select persons to read Scripture, to pray and to meet other pulpit service needs. It also means reminding persons of their important role. It is wise to train as many persons as possible. Everyone needs a chance to serve.

## Job Title: **BIRTHDAY FELLOWSHIP MINISTRY**

**Job Description:** This ministry will prepare birthday fellowship dinners/snacks for new members, which will provide support and nurturing, and to answer any questions that new members might have. It is wise to invite the pastor and/church leaders to this event.

## Job Title: **PRAYER MINISTRY**

**Job Description:** This ministry is responsible for educating the congregation about prayer. Prayer cells may be organized after Sunday morning worship services. This ministry will also recommend periodic prayer workshops and breakfasts for leaders and congregation, oversee Wednesday Evening Prayer Service, and facilitate training of church leaders in conducting a Prayer Service.

## DESCRIPTIONS OF POSSIBLE MINISTRIES UNDER THE YOUTH DEPARTMENT

## Job Title: **BAPTIST YOUTH COUNCIL MINISTRY**

**Job Description:** This ministry will suggest to the ministry Christian educational programs/ activities/ projects that focus on the needs/concerns of youth and help youth to develop their spiritual and leadership abilities.

## Job Title: **YOUTH FELLOWSHIP MINISTRY**

**Job Description:** This ministry will plan and recommend Christian recreational and fun activities/events that will foster greater Christian fellowship and participation among youth in the church and help youth to develop better social skills, build positive friendships, and practice more positive social interaction.

**Job Title**: YOUTH BIBLE FELLOWSHIP MINISTRY LEADER

**Job Description**: Plan and implement a series of Bible studies to help youth understand and apply biblical doctrines to their everyday life situations. Work closely with the Youth Ministry, Baptist Youth Council, and Baptist Youth Fellowship. Assist in the planning of Youth Week, Youth Retreat, and other youth activities. Contribute to the development of the Children's and Youth Worship Service. Assist in planning goals and objectives for the Youth Department.

## POSSIBLE DESCRIPTION FOR THE ADULT MINISTRY

**Job Title: CLUB/AUXILIARY PRESIDENT /MINISTRY**

**Job Description:** Each club leader should seek a purpose for the club that goes beyond just meeting to chat. There may be a mission project for each club and conjunctly a project for the ministry where all clubs work as one.

**Job Title: SUPPORT OPERATIONS DEPARTMENT LEADER**

**Job Description:** This ministry will oversee the equipment for the department, maintaining accurate inventory statements and suggesting equipment to be ordered/repaired. This ministry will provide forms for checking out and receiving equipment. It will also guide the library and bookstore operations.

## SOME SUGGESTED MINISTRIES
1. Basic Membership
   a) New Member's Orientation—both adults and children, separately
   b) Extended Orientation—both adults and children, separately
   c) Big Brothers and Sisters
   d) Lay Participation
   e) Birthday fellowship for parishioners
   f) Prayer Ministry

2. Children's Ministry

3. Youth Ministry

a) Youth Council

b) Youth Fellowship

c) Youth Bible Study

4. Adult Ministry—all clubs/auxiliaries

5. Single Adult Ministry

6. Young Adult Ministry

7. Cultural Enrichment
   a) African Education/History
   b) Theater
   c) Dance
   d) Aids
   e) Health
   f) Physical education

8. Support Ministry
   a) Library
   b) Bookstore
   c) Christian education equipment

## GENERAL EDUCATIONAL MINISTRIES

These ministries may include but are not limited to tutorial, computer, and after-school programs. The important point to remember is that these ministries should not supercede Christian educational ministries. These ministries do help prepare the whole person for serving God.

# Appendix 2
## Sample Evaluation Form for Evaluating Ministry Leaders and Ministry Workers

### Evaluation Form for Ministry Leaders and Ministry Workers

1. Is the leader on time for meetings? Yes or No
2. Is the leader doing a good job? Yes or No
3. Does the leader maintain peaceful relationships with participants? Yes or No

4. Is there good communication between the ministry leader and participants? Yes or No

5. Does the leader accept authoritative assignments? Yes or No

6. Comment on two positive observations of the leader.
   a)
   b)

7. Comment on two observations of the leader that need improvement.
   a)
   b)

Signature of observer: _____

Name of person observed_____

Name of ministry: _____

Date: _____

# Appendix 3
## Sample Get-to-Know You Form
## for Department Leaders

### INTRODUCTION FORM FOR LEADERS

1. Your name _____
2. Your address _____
3. Your home phone _____
4. Your home fax _____
5. Your work phone _____
6. Name of ministry _____
7. Tell me about your experience and/or desired experience for this ministry.
8. Discuss your past experiences associated with this ministry.
9. What are your special skills, gifts and talents?
10. What in particular do you desire to do in this ministry?

# Appendix 4

## Sample Meeting Agenda for Training New Department Leaders, Directors and Ministry Leaders

### SUGGESTED AGENDA FOR TRAINING NEW DEPARTMENT LEADERS

1. Prayer
2. Welcome and completing introduction form
3. Review department handbook or "guidelines"
4. Job description
5. Adhering to schedule
6. Decide at least three times to meet with your ministry leaders. Also, ask your ministry leaders to meet on their own.
7. Requisitions (requesting funds or services)
   a) Food
   b) General
   c) Speakers—attach bio
   d) Workshops—attach workshop topics. Each workshop leader should submit an outline at least two weeks before scheduled workshop.
   e) Posters/flyers
   f) Completing a requisition for ministry funds
   g) Fund raising
8. Bulletin Boards
9. Field trips requests:
   Place
   Purpose
   Anticipated learning experience
   Overnight/late returns/insurance
10. Review and sign off for manual or department guidelines

# Appendix 5

## Suggested Agenda for First Department Leader's Meeting with Ministry Leaders and Ministry Workers

Note: A secretary should be elected to take minutes at all meetings. Typed minutes should be provided to the department leader. The department leader should provide a copy to the DCE.

1. Devotions and introductions
2. Purpose of meeting—To begin planning for the year.
3. A get-to-know-you game or ice-breaker
4. Distribute a copy of the upcoming annual calendar and budget
5. Discuss goals for the ministry.
6. Distribute and collect surveys
7. Begin planning. Either the team or groups of threes work on planning for the year. Follow the calendar. One group may be responsible for three months, etc. In the end all leaders and workers will share in the planning. Allow about one hour for this session. Then ask each group to meet on their own before the next meeting to prepare their recommendations.
8. Ask for ways to evangelize (to spread the news to the community and ways for inviting new participants to the ministry); write down suggestions and share with the Minister of Education.
9. Review or establish at least two ministry meeting dates for all ministry leaders to meet with the department leader.
10. The Ministry group prays.
11. Discuss expectations of ministry leaders—All details should clearly tell what will take place. **Detail plans: including program, flyers, bulletins, should be presented to the DCE one month prior to your event. A late plan** may cause a cancellation of the event or activity. Keep in mind **plans may be approved, approved with suggestions, or not approved** with specified reasons. **Field trip** requests must be submitted two months in advance to be considered. We, the **sponsor,** must **secure policy on insurance** and **liability** and receive "release forms" for field trips. **Requisitions** for **space** or **funds** must be submitted **one month** before the event

or the requisition **will be returned** and the **event will be canceled.** Fund-raising: Some churches strictly tithe, which I suggest, others will allow some or all groups to fund raise. Discuss with your DCE.

12. Ask ministry leaders to share some fun things they liked last year.
13. Remind leaders of teamwork. Each member plays a part in the ministry.
14. Speakers and workshop leaders—names of speakers and workshop leaders and preachers for the entire year will be approved by the DCE.
15. Field trips and workshops—All field trips and workshops should have: a purpose, learning experience, and relate to our ministry.
16. Discuss what should take place at each meeting: activity, learning, etc.
17. Announce next meeting date.
18. Benediction

# Appendix 6

## Suggested Agenda for Second Department Leader's Meeting with Ministry Leaders and Workers

1. Devotions
2. Ice breaker
3. Review minutes from last time.
4. Discuss survey results.
5. Work on annual planning—**Decide on all details—Who will be responsible for what and suggest deadlines for assignments.** All assignments, planning for trips, speakers, workshop leaders, should be completed within one month. A draft should be typed and given to the department leader. The department leader provides a copy to the DCE. Upon approval or modification, the department leader will meet with the team to complete planning.
6. Select prayer partners—select two or three to be prayer partners for the year. Discuss responsibilities.
7. The ministry group prays.
8. Announce next meeting.
9. Benediction

# Appendix 7

## Suggested Agenda for Third Department Leader's Meeting with Ministry Leaders and Ministry Workers

1. Devotions
2. Discuss concerns and reviews of the DCE.
3. Final suggestions
4. Copy of final plans
5. Ministry team prays
6. Review the calendar
7. Benediction

# Appendix 8

## Evaluation Form for Board Members

1. Is the leader on time for meetings? Yes or No
2. Is the leader doing a good job? Yes or No
3. Does the leader maintain peaceful relationships with participants? Yes or No
4. Is there good communication between the ministry leader and participants? Yes or No
5. Does the leader accept authoritative assignments? Yes or No
6. Comment on two positive observations of the leader.
   a)
   b)
7. Comment on two observations of the leader that need improvement.
   a)
   b)

Signature of observer: _____

Name of the person observed: _____

Name of ministry: _____

# Appendix 9

## Goals for Department Leader(s)

Name of Department: _____

Name of Department Leader: _____

Name of Ministry leaders:_____

_____

Date report completed: _____

Per your vision, after prayer,

1. What would you like to happen in this ministry?
   Think about:
   a) what is happening at this church in this ministry.
   b) what should be happening at this church in this ministry.
   c) what needs commonly exist with this age group.
   d) what ideas will help members of this ministry become
   more spiritual and meet the needs of the whole person.
2. Goals decided upon by the team
   a)
   b)
   c)
   d)
   e)

Note: The Department leader may ask ministry leaders for their goals.

## Department Leaders—Attach a Copy of This Sheet to Each Submitted Annual Ministry Plan.

Department: _____

Department Leader: _____

Ministry Leaders:_____

_____

Date of completing plan:_____

After prayer and careful review of the plans from the ministry leader, the following may be considered:

1. What I suggest to be deleted and why
   a)
   b)
   c)

2. What I suggest to be added and why
   a)
   b)
   c)

3. Other Suggestions

4. Where I think the ministry is headed and why

# Appendix 10

## Christian Education Evaluation Form for Workshop Leaders

### Please Circle Your Response

1. Was the leader prepared?      Yes   No

2. Did the leader provide new information for you?      Yes   No

3. Do you feel you have been spiritually fed?     Yes   No

4. Did the leader allow you to participate in the discussion?
   Yes   No

5. How would you rate the workshop leader's content?
   Excellent        Good            Fair            Poor

6. Would you like for the leader to provide another workshop for the future?  Yes  No

7. How would you rate the workshop leader's ability to be clearly understood?  Excellent      Good      Fair        Poor

8. Was the workshop leader energetic (had enthusiasm about the subject)?        Yes  No

9. Did the workshop leader provide new insights for you? Yes   No

10. Write any comments or suggestions you have about this work-shop. _____

_____

_____

11. Name other workshops that you desire to attend to help you grow spiritually.

_____

_____

# Appendix 11

## Suggested Board of Christian Education Meeting Agenda

1. Devotional
2. Minutes
3. Board members comments or overviews about their ministry (prefer handouts to save time)
4. Board discussions and forming subcommittees

   EXAMPLES
   a) Teacher training
   b) Evaluations
   c) Sunday school calendar review, e.g., VBS, retreats, school opening and progress, need for teachers, review of Sunday school literature, and any other pertinent Sunday school items
   d) Quarterly calendar from all departments
   e) Board calendar review
   f) Special concerns: deaths/sickness in connected families
   g) Other concerns
5. Fifteen minutes prayer time in small groups and collectively
6. Final business and announcements
7. Benediction

# Bibliography

*A Manual for Leadership Education and Curriculum Guide.* Nashville: Sunday School Publishing Board, 1994.

Atchibald, H. A. "Curriculum" in *Harper's Encyclopedia.* Cully, Iris V. and Kendig Burbaker, editors. Second edition. San Francisco: Harper and Row, 1971.

Azevedo, Mario, editor. *Africana Studies—A Survey of Africa and the African Diaspora* Durham: Carolina Academic Press, 1993.

*Behavior.* Trenton, New Jersey: African World Press, Inc., 1994.

Birchette, Colleen. "A History of Religious Education in the Black Church." in *Urban Church Education* Edited by Donald B. Rogers. Birmingham: Religious Education Press, 1989.

Blackwell, John A. *The Black Church and the Black Experience.* Nashville: United Methodist Publishing House, 1971.

Blazier, D. Kenneth, & Isham, R. Linda. *The Teaching Church at Work —A Manual for the Board of Christian Education.* Valley Forge: Judson Press, 1993.

Bond, Horace Mann. "Main Currents in the Educational Crisis Affecting Afro-Americans." *Freedom Ways.* 8:3 (Fall, 1968), 305.

Boylan, Anne M. *Sunday School—The Formation of an American Institution, 1790-1880.* New Haven: Yale University Press, 1988.

Brackney, William Henry. *The Baptists* New York: Greenwood Press, 1988.

Brochure: First Baptist Church, Petersburg, Virginia. "Some Interesting Accounts of the Sunday School of the First Baptist Church."

Brochure: Second Presbyterian Church "Please Count Me In Too"—Brochure-Katy Ferguson House.

Brochure: First Baptist Church—"Celebrating More Than 200 Years of Christian Witness."

Brown, Hallie Q. "Homespun Heroines and Other Women of Distinction" in *Cubberly's History of Education*. Xenia, Ohio: Aldine Publishing Company, 1922.

Brown, Lorenzo Quincy. "The Study of the Sunday School—Provided for the Immediate Department of the Colored Methodist Episcopal Church," Thesis Howard University, June 1940, pp. 1-4.

Bernstein, Alvin. *How to Develop a Department of Christian Education Within the Local Church*. Nashville: Townsend Press, 1995.

Bucke, Emory Stevens, editor. *The History of American Methodism*, Vol.1. Nashville: Abingdon Press, 1964.

Bullock, Henry. *A History of Negro Education in the South—From 1619 to the Present*. Cambridge, Massachusetts: Harvard University Press, 1967.

Bultmann, William A. *British Humanitarianism*. Edited by Samuel McCulloch. New York: The Church Historical Society, 1950.

Carruthers, Jacob H. "The Wisdom of Governance in Kemet." in *Kemet and the African Worldview—Research, Rescue, and Restoration*. Los Angeles: University of Sankore Press, 1986.

*Christian Education Journal*. "Analyzing the Curriculum Debate." 13:3. (Spring, 1993): 95.

Cloud, Olivia. *Sunday School Growth*. Nashville: Convention Press—The Sunday School Board of the Southern Baptist, 1990.

_____ "Historical Perspectives on the Growth Oriented Sunday School," *Black Baptist Sunday School Growth*, compiled by Olivia Cloud. Nashville: Convention Press, 1990.

Cully, Iris V. *The Bible in Christian Education*. Minneapolis: Augsburg Fortress Press, 1995.

Cully, Iris, et al. *Harper's Encyclopedia of Religious Education*. New York: Harper and Row, 1990.

Davidson, Basil. *Africa in History*. New York: Collier Books, 1974.

Diop, Cheikh Anta. *The African Origin of Civilization*. Mercer Cook, Editor. Chicago: Lawrence Hill Books, 1974.

Edwards, Lonzy. "Religion Education by Blacks During Reconstruction," *Religious Education*. 69: (July-August, 1974), 413-416.

Fitts, Leroy. *A History of Black Baptists*. Nashville: Broadman Press, 1985.

Franklin, John Hope. *From Slavery to Freedom: A History of Negro Americans*, Third Edition. New York: Alfred A. Knopf, 1967.

Franklin, John Hope and Alfred A. Moss, Jr. "The Effort to Attain Peace" in *From Slavery to Freedom—A History of African Americans*, seventh edition. New York: McGraw-Hill, Inc., 1994.

Frazier, Edward Franklin. *The Negro Church in America*, New York: Schocken Books, 1974.

Gaines, Wesley. *African Methodism in the South*. Atlanta: Franklin Publishing House, 1890.

Gangel, Kenneth. *Building Leaders for Church Education*. Chicago. Chicago: Moody Press, 1970.

Gibbs, James L. Jr. editor. *Peoples of Africa*. Chicago: Holt, Rinehart and Winston Inc., 1965.

Greene, Lorenzo J. *Working with Carter G. Woodson—The Father of Black History—A Diary of 1928-1930*. Baton Rouge: Louisiana State University Press, 1989.

Grinstead, S. E., Sr., "Katie Ferguson, Pioneer in the Sunday School Movement," Published by the Sunday School Publishing Board of the National Baptists Convention, U.S.A. Inc., Folder.

Harman, Nolan. *Encyclopedia of World Methodism*. Vol. 1. Nashville: United Methodist Publishing House, 1974.

Harris, James. Independent Presbyterian Records by the First African Baptist Church. Savannah , Georgia, 1925.

Harris, Maria and Moran, Grabriel. *Reshaping Religious Education Conversations on Contemporary Practice*. Louisville: Westminster John Knox Press,1998

Hayes, Edward L. "The Biblical Foundations of Christian Education" in *Introduction to Biblical Christian Education*. Werner Graendorf, editor. Chicago: Moody Press, 1981.

Hilliard, Asa III. "Kemetics Concepts in Education" in *Egypt Child of Africa* edited by Ivan Van Sertima. New Brunswick: Transaction Publishers, 1994.

_____ *Egypt Child of Africa*, edited by Ivan Van Sertima. New Brunswick: Transactional Publishers, 1995.

_____*The Maroon Within Us*. Baltimore: Black Classic Press, 1995.

*History of Education*. Xenia, Ohio: Aldine Publishing Company, 1922.

Hodges, Sloan, compiler. Brochure "Black Baptists in American and the Origins of Their Conventions." D.C.: Progressive National Baptist Convention, Inc.

Howard, Phillip E. *Sunday Schools—The World Around*. The Official Report of the World's Fifth Sunday School Convention, 1907.

Ivan, Van Sertima. New Brunswick: Transaction Publishers, 1994.

Johnson, Benjamin. "God's Viewpoint of Christian Education," *The Christian Education Informer*. 50:1. (June-August, 1997), 21.

Johnson, Lin. "Understanding and Using Curriculum." in *Christian Education: Foundations for the Future*, Robert E. Clark, et al, editors. Chicago: Moody Press, 1991.

*Joint Educational Manual—Black Perspectives in Church Education*, "Role and function of Resources."

Jones, Charles. *Religious Instruction of the Negroes in the United States*. New York: Kraus Reprint Company, 1969.

Karenga, Maulana and Jacob H. Carruthers. *Kemet and the African Worldview-Research, Rescue and Restoration*. Los Angeles: University of Sankore Press, 1986.

Karenga, Maulana. "Restoration of the Husia: Reviving a Sacred Legacy" in *Kemet and the African Worldview: Research, Rescue and Restoration*. Los Angeles: University of Sankore Press, 1986.

Kellar, Marcel. *Building a Strong Sunday Church School*. Nashville: National Baptist Publishing Board, 1987.

Knight, Edward, editor. *A Documentary History of Education in the South Before 1860*. Chapel Hill: The University of North Carolina Press, 1950.

Lincoln, Eric C. *Race, Religion, and the Continuing American Dilemma*. New York: Hill and Wang, 1984.

Loetcher, Lefferts. *A Brief History of the Presbyterians*. Philadelphia: The Wesdminster Press, 1958.

Lossing, Benson. *Eminent Americans*. New York: Mason Brothers, 1857.

Love, Mary A. "Musings on the Sunday School in the Black Community" in *Renewing the Sunday School and the CCD*, edited by D. Campbell Wyckoff. Birmingham: Religious Education Press, 1986.

Lubicz, Isha De Schwalller. *Her-Bak— The Living Face of Ancient Egypt*. New York: Inner Traditions International LTD, 1978.

Lynn, Robert W. and Elliott Wright. *The Big Little School—Two Hundred Years of the Sunday School*. New York: Harper and Row, 1971.

Marimba, Ani. *Yurugu: An African Centered Critique of European Cultural Thought and Behavior.* Trenton, New York: Harper and Row, 1971.

Marlow, Joe D. "Choosing Appropriate Curricular Models for Christian Education" in *Christian Education Journal*. 15:2. Winter, 1995.

Minter, Thomas and Alfred Prettyman. *Encyclopedia of African American Culture and History, Volume 2*. New York: Simon and Schuster Macmillan, 1996.

Moore, Nellie B. "Developing Christian Education in the Local Church" in *The Christian Education Informer.* Sunday School Publishing Board. 51: 3. ( December 98- Feb 1999), 21.

Morris, Calvin. "African Americans and Methodism" in *Directory of African American Religious Bodies—A Compendium by Howard University School of Divinity*. Edited by Payne, Wardell. D.C.: Howard University Press, 1991.

Mott, E. *Narratives of Colored Americans*. New York: Bowne, 1882.

News Release "A Cincinnati News Press," June 5, 1947.

News Release *The New York Amsterdam News*, Saturday, June 21, 1947.

News Release *Philadelphia Tribune*, June 7, 1947.

News Release *Second Presbyterian Church*—New York, New York.

News Release *The New York Lines*, June 7, 1947.

Nieman, Donald G. *To Set the Law in Motion—The Freedmen's Bureau and the Legal Rights of Blacks 1865-1868*. Millwood, New York: KTO Press, 1979.

Pamphlet "When an Editor Looks at Content." Nashville: Graded Press—United Methodist Publishing Board, revised 1988.

Payne, Daniel. *History of the A.M.E. Church*. Nashville: Publishing House of the Sunday School Union, 1891.

Powell, Grady. Interview, June 10, 1993, Pastor of Gillfield Baptist Church. Petersburg. *Pulpit Helps* .16: (November 1990).

Reid, Ira. "The Development of Adult Education for Negroes in the United States," *Journal of Negro Education*. 14:3 (Summer 1945), 200.

*Religious Education Teaching Approaches*. Australia: Queensland: Curriculum Services Branch, Department of Education, 1987.

Report developed during Krisheim II Conference on Education Resources for Black Churches August 31—September 3, 1970, sponsored by the Black Christian Education Administrative and Coordinating Committee.

Rogers, Alain. "The A.M.E. Church : A Study in Black Nationalism" in *The Black Church*. 1:1 (1975).

Rogers, Donald B. *Urban Church Education*. Birmingham: Religious Education Press, 1989.

Rogers, Donald. *Urban Church Education*. Colleen Birchett in "History of Religious Education in the Black Church." Birmingham: Religious Education Press, 1989.

Schindler, Claude E., Jr.. "Planning and Achieving Curricular Excellence" in *Christian Education Journal*. Scripture Press Ministries. 9:1. Autumn, 1988.

Seymour, Jack L. "Approaches to Christian Education" in *Mapping Christian Education—Approaches to Congregational Learning*. Nashville: Abingdon Press, 1997.

Seymour, Jack. *From Sunday School to Church School—Continuities in Protestant Church Education in the United Stated, 1860-1929*. D.C.: University Press of America, 1982.

Shipley, Anthony J. "Choosing and Using Resources in the Black Church." Prepared by the Department of Youth Publications, Section on Curriculum Resources, Board of Discipleship of the United Methodist Church—Published by Graded Press, 1973.

Shockley, Grant S. *Christian Education Journey of Black Americans—Past, Present, Future*. Nashville: Discipleship Resources, 1985.

Smith, Jessie Carney, editor. *Black Firsts—2,000 Years of Extraordinary Achievement*. Detroit: Visible Ink Press, 1994.

Smith, Jessie. *Statistical Record of Blacks in America*. 4th edition. Detroit: Gale Research, 1997.

Smith, Sid. *Reaching the Black Community Through the Sunday School*. Nashville: Sunday School Board of Southern Baptist Church Convention, 1984.

_____ *Reaching the Black Community Through the Sunday School*. Nashville: Convention Press, 1988.

_____. 10 Super Sunday Schools in the Black Community.

Spencer, Ruth L. and Idris W. Jones. *The Work of the Sunday School Superintendent*. Valley Forge: Judson Press, 1994.

Stafford, Tim. "This Little Light of Mine." *Christianity Today*. (October 8, 1990).

Steward, Austin. "Termination of Slavery" in *Lift Every Voice—African American Oratory, 1787-1900*. Edited by Philip S. Foner and Robert Branham. Tuscaloosa: The University of Alabama Press, 1998.

Sunday School Publishing Board. *Sunday School Informer.* Nashville: (February, 1934).

Telephone conversation with Historian Stanley Lemons of First Baptist Church, Providence, Rhode Island and telephone conversation with Dr. Robert.

Telephone conversation with pastor of Second Presbyterian Church, New York, New York, fall 1990.

Telephone Interview and written response. Dickerson, Dennis, Historiographer for A.M.E. Williamstown, Massachusetts, March 26, 1993.

Telephone interview with Deacon Harry James of First African Baptist Church, Savannah Georgia, 1993.

The Christian Education Department. *A Manual for Leadership Education and Curriculum Guide.* Nashville: Sunday School Publishing Board NBC, USA, Inc, 1994.

Thomas, Latta. *Biblical Faith and the Black American*. Valley Forge: Judson Press, 1981.

Thomas, Edgar. *The First African Baptist Church in North America.*

Tyms, James. *The Rise of Religious Education Among Negro Baptists*. D.C.: University Press, 1979.

Walker, Wyatt T. "Fifth Anniversary-History Brochure" and 2/93 telephone conversation with Dr. Grady Davis and viewing the Heritage Room of Gillfield Baptist Church with Deacons Mrs. Lula E. Allgood and Mrs. Thomassine M. Burke.

Walz, L. Humphrey. " Excerpts from Sermon, June 8, 1947. Pastor of Second Presbyterian Baptist Church.

Washington, Booker Taliaferro. *Up from Slavery*. New York: Doubleday and Company, 1971.

Wesley, Charles H. and Patricia Romero. *Negro Americans in the Civil War—From Slavery to Citizenship*. New York: Publishers Company, Inc. Under the Association for the Study of Negro Life and History, 1968.

Wilmore, Gayraud and James Cone. *Black Theology: A Documentary History, 1966-1979*. Maryknoll, New York: Orbis Books, 1979.

Woodson, Carter G. *The Education of the Negro Prior to 1861*. Washington, D.C.: The Association for the Study of Negro Life and History, 1919.

Woodson, Carter. *African Background Outlined*. New York Negro Universities Press, 1936.

Wright, David W. "Choosing Appropriate Curricular Models for Christian Education" in *Christian Education Journal*. 15:2. Winter, 1995.

Wyckoff, D. Campbell. *Renewing the Sunday School and the CCD*. Birmingham: Religious Education Press, 1986.

# About the Author

Rev. Dr. Oneal C. Sandidge is author of *Teacher Training in the African American Church* and *I'm Stuck! Help Me Start a Youth Ministry in the African American Church.* Dr. Sandidge is a member, licensed and ordained, of Timothy Baptist Church in Amherst, Virginia where Rev. William Glover, Jr., is pastor.

He has published numerous scholarly articles. Dr. Sandidge served as Associate Professor of Christian Education at Beulah Heights Bible College in Atlanta and Luther Rice Seminary in Lithonia, Georgia.

He holds a bachelor's degree in religion and elementary education from Lynchburg College, a private institution; two masters: Columbia University and Howard University Divinity School; a doctorate in ministry from Drew University; Merrill's Fellow at Harvard University and a Piedmont Virginia Writing Fellow at Virginia State University. He has taken course work at Virginia Union and the University of Virginia.

He has served as a DCE in a church with about 4,000 members in Harlem, New York, where he was responsible for thirty-five ministries, seventy-five Sunday school teachers, and a large Sunday school department.

Dr. Sandidge enjoys teaching secondary English, conducting national professional workshops, serving as adjunct Christian education professor at Defiance College in Ohio, and Trinity Episcopal Seminary in Pennsylvania, and serving as a consultant to churches in Christian education.

He is the son of Hattie Dawson and the late Wardie Sandidge.